Now You Can Play Guitar

The Moon Rose Guitar Program
by
Pauric Mather

authorHOUSE

1663 Liberty Drive, Suite 200
Bloomington, Indiana 47403
(800) 839-8640
www.AuthorHouse.com

© 2006 Pauric Mather. All rights reserved.

No part of this book may be reproduced, stored in a retrieval system, or transmitted by any means without the written permission of the author.

First published by AuthorHouse 6/9/2006

ISBN: 1-4208-9656-3 (sc)

Printed in the United States of America
Bloomington, Indiana

This book is printed on acid-free paper.

This book copyright © 2005 Pauric Mather / Moon Rose Music Limited.
International copyright secured. All rights reserved.
Unauthorized reproduction of all or part of this book by any means including scanning and photocopying is an infringement of copyright.
THE MOON ROSE GUITAR PROGRAM
Copyright © 2002
Pauric Mather / Kevin Mather / Moon Rose Music Limited.
International Copyright Secured. All Rights Reserved.
THE MOON ROSE POCKET GUITAR
Copyright © 1996
Pauric Mather / Kevin Mather / Moon Rose Music Limited.
International Copyright Secured. All Rights Reserved.

All the guitar lessons in this book have been written and engraved exactly the same as taught in "The Moon Rose Guitar Program". It is now regarded by many to be the most successful way of both learning and teaching guitar in the world today. They are completely relevant to all songs on both electric and acoustic guitar. They have also been carefully laid out to minimize page turning, and the important points emboldened, making it easier to read from a distance. This is the first guitar book ever published to incorporate teaching and learning techniques from " The Moon Rose Visual Guitar Teaching System" (MVT). Learning guitar and playing music from this book will be a pleasure, and a unique musical experience.

ACKNOWLEDGEMENTS

Flor Crowley, Andy Foley, Andy Heffernan, and Claire Carroll; Kildare; The quiet angels.
Finbar Furey and Sheila Furey.
George Furey; For showing me things not known to kings.
Maud Nolan, Naas, Reike Master; Without whose help this book would not have been possible.
John and Joy Mullen, Los Christianos, Tenerife; Two very special people.
Kevin Mather; Managing Director. Moon Rose Guitar Academy.
Darren Mac Namara; National Irish Bank.
Blaise Brosnan; Management Resource Institute.
Paula Curran; Coda Music Technology, Ireland.
Tom Denver; For the Denver strategy.
Dick Mather and Weldon Mather.
Aidan and Lynette McCullough
Sean Hall; Cill Dara Security. For invaluable support.
Pat Mather; Far away but close.
Michelle Lynch; Thanks for the hand.
Ettie Mather, Noreen Phelan, and Stella Lunny; for all the help with Moon Rose Guitar Academy.
Maureen Whyte; Always the heart. Bijou for you.
Walter and Mary Hennessy; HMD Music Limited.
Dolly Garvey and Noel Collender; Naas; For all the help with our classes and workshops.
Pat O Sullivan; Killorglin, Co. Kerry; For the legend of John Sean Bawn.
John Gallagher; London; Another Daytimer.
Mark and Julianne Hennessy; Hollywood Hills, California. Now you'll be able to play piano and guitar Mark.
Gavin Ralstan and Alan Grundy; Two of the great guitar teachers.
Bill and Bobs friends all over the world; Just for today.
Paddy Power; Naas, For helping to create "The Moon Rose Visual Guitar Teaching System" (MVT). Thank You Paddy.
Bill O Connor and Rob O Connell; Millbrook Press Limited.
Victor Murphy; Celbridge and USA; Hope you are still playing guitar Vic.
Daniel Cooke; Authorhouse, UK
Jennifer Brandt; Authorhouse, USA

And finally
Every one of you who attended my classes and workshops over the years *(and that's a lot)*. Thank you all for your time and for giving me the privilege of teaching you. We all got better and better day by day. Now we are all guitar players. You taught me one of the greatest lessons of all. No one of us is better or worse than the next person on guitar. Even if it's your first day to play. We're just different, that's all.

ABOUT THE AUTHOR

Pauric Mather started playing guitar when he was seven years old. He was already teaching guitar by the time he was nineteen when living in Hammersmith, West London. During the twenty years that followed his teaching and writing skills became highly specialized. He is a pioneer of new ideas in the field of guitar teaching and learning, with which he has achieved remarkable success. All of his ground breaking work is based on a life of personal experience, working with not hundreds, but thousands of people who wanted to, and succeeded in playing guitar. He also founded World Guitar Day in 2004.

Today, still in what he describes as "a magical adventure" Pauric Mather is teaching with the same enthusiasm as when he first started. Based in Dublin, Ireland, his schools, workshops, and masterclasses are attended by people of all ages, nationalities, and walks of life. They are all realizing their dream of becoming competent guitar players.

There are no short cuts to anywhere worth going. There are no short cuts in this book. Instead Pauric Mathers vast experience enables him to multi-task as he writes and teaches. This dramatically increases the speed of your progress. Very few teachers in the world are capable of this and he uses it to great effect in this book. There is no compromise either. Everything is shown to you exactly as played by professional guitarists.

His unique and innovative teaching skills and vast experience has also enabled him to create 'The Moon Rose Guitar Program". Because of its success he is now regarded as one of the leading guitar teachers in the world today.

Pauric Mather is also an international author. His unique style enables him to write songbooks for international recording artists, most notably "The Finbar Furey Songbook" in 2002. This book created a sensation within music publishing. It was the first book ever published to combine guitar boxes with picture chords and tuning guides. With his vast teaching experience Pauric Mather was very much aware of the advantages this would give to anyone who wanted to learn from song books. His methods are now being accepted, and implemented by many other schools and publishers. He constantly receives emails commenting on how much easier it is to learn from his books and unique writing style, compared to most others.

His approach to learning guitar is remarkable in its simplicity. It is based on three very simple but practical steps. In the early weeks of learning the best results are achieved by
1, working with the fretting hand on its own,
2, the rhythm hand on its own, and
3, then playing with both hands together.

His approach to learning a song on guitar is also based on three simple, yet very practical steps.
1, Good sound,
2, Good rhythm, and
3, Quick chord/note changing.

Believe it or not that is all any song is on guitar. If you practice each step individually, then your chances of success are greatly increased when you put them together, in other words play a song.

During his lifetime Pauric Mather has to date worked with over 10,000 students, teaching guitar to the highest possible standards.
On the basis that only a well informed person can write a well informed book, he is the ideal person to write a teach yourself guitar book.

THIS BOOK IS ABOUT YOU

BY PAURIC MATHER

ITS GOAL IS SIMPLE!..........................TO HELP YOU REACH YOURS

This book is not about the guitar. It does not contain sheet music. It doesn't have one song. It has the guitar skills that you need to play every song that ever was, or will be played on guitar. This book is about you. That is the big difference between The Moon Rose Guitar Program and all other learning methods. It is totally focused on you from start to finish. Here are just a few examples;

SHEET MUSIC IS NOT MUSIC
IT IS ONLY INK ON PAPER

Have a quick flick through this book. You will not find one note of sheet music or guitar tablature anywhere. If you wanted to learn to read music there are plenty of books available. If you want to play guitar I want to help you play guitar, not read music. Most guitarists never learn to read scored music.

In reality sheet music is not music. It is only ink on paper. Music is the sound that comes from your guitar or any musical instrument. Isn't it a well known fact that some of the greatest artists the world has ever known couldn't read music? Why did they succeed? They were playing guitar. I rest my case. Yet we buy books that promise to teach us guitar and almost immediately we end up being shown how to read music instead.

In the beginning most of us want to learn guitar for personal pleasure, or to get competent enough to play at parties and sing songs. More of us want to be able to play with a friend, in a local group, choir, or band. You do not need to read music in order to achieve any of these goals. Maybe later in your career if you want to work in orchestras, recording studios, or teach guitar, you might consider learning to read music.

Your guitar won't change either. It may be in your bedroom or in a shop waiting for you to buy it. One thing is for sure. It will still be the same the next time you pick it up as it is today. So there isn't much point in writing about the guitar either. That is not what a teach yourself guitar book is for. Do we want to learn about the guitar or do we want to learn how to play the guitar?

You don't play songs and then learn to play guitar. It's not possible. You learn to play guitar and then you play songs. Once you become a competent guitarist you can learn and play any song you like especially now with so many song books and the internet available to us. Why is this? The answer is simple. Even though all songs are different the guitar skills needed to play them are the very same. There is only one right way to play and that is then applied to all songs.

That is why this book is not about the guitar. Its does not contain sheet music either. It does not contain one song. In time you will come to realize that it contains a million songs or more, and can be used as a constant companion to all other guitar song books.

I refuse to play songs I don't like. I don't expect you to either. It is my personal experience thousands of times over that the best results are achieved by focusing on your hands, your ears, your imagination, and the actual fingering skills that you need to play guitar. Then you will have the freedom to play any song you like.
That's what the Moon Rose Guitar Program is all about.

LUCYS LETTER

Pauric,

    What a wonderful book! It is so informative, interesting and so well written I could not leave it down. I felt I wanted to play guitar. You explained each thing so simply and so well that I wanted to turn over to the next page to see what else you had written. I want to wish you all the best and in my opinion it should be a number one best seller.

Good Luck and God Bless.
Lucy Power
Naas,
County Kildare,
Ireland.

HE DIDN'T REALLY BELIEVE HE COULD PLAY GUITAR

(AND LOOK WHAT HAPPENED)

BY SEAMUS Mc KENNA

Pauric Mather
Musical Director
Moon Rose Guitar Academy
Moon Rose House
34 The Paddocks
Naas
County Kildare

Kildare Town
Co Kildare
31st July 2003

Dear Pauric,

I just felt that I should drop you a note to express my appreciation and amazement for the fact that I now play the guitar. I know you told me that your teaching methods would work for anyone but forgive me Pauric because I didn't really believe you. I only attended your classes to encourage my son to attend. I knew that learning to play music was not as simple as having the desire to learn. I had previously tried to learn the tin whistle and the bodhran when I was much younger but without success. The teachers I used had concluded that "I didn't have it". Thanks to you I now know that it was them who "didn't have it", not me.

You didn't have a lot to work with in me. A 58 year old business man who couldn't spare a lot of time to practice and who didn't believe it could possibly work anyway. On the other had I did really want to be able to play. From that very first lesson my disbelief began to wither. I went home clutching my Beginners Guitar Book and told my wife that I was going to learn how to play the guitar. After only one year it has actually come to pass and your simple step by step guidance has made it all seem so easy.

Now I konw I am nowhere near being you most successful student and indeed could be in with a shout for the least successful slot. Eric Clapton doesn't have to worry about me putting him in the shade. My son, who needs less practice but has more time at his disposal, has progrssed to the point where he comfortable playing onstage and is now writing his own songs. I am however equal to anyone in the pleasure I get from my music. Playing guitar has become my number one hobby. Roll on retirement. I can't wait.

Thanks a lot

Seamus McKenna

THE

MOON ROSE

GUITAR
PROGRAM

CONTENTS

ACKNOWLEDGEMENTS	V
ABOUT THE AUTHOR	VI
THIS BOOK IS ABOUT YOU	VII
HE DIDN'T REALLY BELIEVE HE COULD PLAY GUITAR	X

WEEK ONE   LESSON ONE

BAD THUMB POSITIONING BEHIND THE NECK.	2
NOT STRENGTHENING YOUR WEAKER THIRD, AND FOURTH FINGERS.	2
LEARNING G CHORD THE WRONG WAY	2
LEARNING RHYTHMS THE WRONG WAY	2

WEEK TWO   LESSON TWO

WHAT IS A SONG ON GUITAR	6
AM I LEFT HANDED OR RIGHT HANDED	8
WHAT IS THE BEST TYPE OF GUITAR TO LEARN ON	8
WHAT TO LOOK FOR WHEN BUYING A GUITAR	8
WHAT ELSE WILL I NEED	9
WHAT TYPE OF PLECTRUM SHOULD I USE	9

WEEK THREE   LESSON THREE

A POCKET GUITAR	13
UNDERSTANDING THE FRETBOARD AND STRINGS	17
FOR GUITAR TEACHERS	17
A CAPO WHAT DO I NEED THAT FOR?	18
PRACTICE MAKES PERFECT…….RUBBISH.	19

WEEK FOUR   LESSON FOUR

GOOD POSTURE / GOOD SET UP / HOLDING YOUR GUITAR / AN INVISIBLE SKILL	22
POSTURE CHECK	23
ALL GREAT GUITAR PLAYING STARTS HERE	25
YOUR WEAK FINGERS AND HOW TO STRENGTHEN THEM	30
SOME OF THE INVISIBLE SKILLS OF GREAT GUITAR PLAYING	36
WHAT MANY TEACHING METHODS FORGET TO TELL YOU, BUT SHOULD	37
THE MOST IMPORTANT CHORD YOU WILL EVER LEARN ON GUITAR	38

WEEK FIVE   LESSON FIVE

A SIMPLE BUT AMAZING PRACTICE TECHNIQUE	43
THE BEST WAY TO STRUM A GUITAR	43
START DEVELOPING YOUR LISTENING SKILLS NOW	44
MOON ROSE GUITAR PRACTICE PROGRAM WEEK FIVE	46

WEEK SIX   LESSON SIX

THE BEST WAY TO LEARN GUITAR CHORDS	48
BUILDING A FOUNDATION TO GREAT GUITAR PLAYING	48
GUITAR SKILLS THAT WILL LAST A LIFETIME	49
WHAT IS E MINOR, MAJOR, M7, MAJ7, 7, SUS4, WHAT DO THEY MEAN?	50
THE NEXT THREE MOST IMPORTANT CHORDS ON GUITAR	52
MOON ROSE GUITAR PRACTICE PROGRAM WEEK SIX	56

WEEK SEVEN   LESSON SEVEN

LEARN G CHORD THE RIGHT WAY	60
A QUESTION THAT I HAVE BEEN ASKED A THOUSAND TIMES	64
HERE IS A GUIDING PRINCIPLE FOR LIFE	64
PLAYING YOUR GUITAR WITHOUT LOOKING AT IT	65
MOON ROSE GUITAR PRACTICE PROGRAM WEEK SEVEN	67

WEEK EIGHT   LESSON EIGHT

RHYTHM GUITAR	70
ALL GUITAR RHYTHMS START HERE	70
THE WRONG WAY TO LEARN GUITAR RHYTHMS	71
THE RIGHT WAY TO LEARN GUITAR RHYTHMS	71
THE SECRET IT IS SO SIMPLE YOU WILL MISS IT. MOST DO.	71
GUITAR RHYTHMS YOU CAN USE IN THOUSANDS OF SONGS	72
MOON ROSE PRACTICE PROGRAM WEEK EIGHT	76

WEEK NINE   LESSON NINE

ANOTHER SECRET	78
THE AMATEUR APPROACH	78
THE PROFESSIONAL APPROACH	78
ALL LEAD GUITAR AND FINGERSTYLE GUITAR ALSO STARTS HERE.	82
A SIMPLE BUT INVALUABLE RHYTHM HAND EXERCISE	84
MOON ROSE GUITAR PRACTICE PROGRAM WEEK NINE	86

WEEK TEN   LESSON TEN

A SIMPLE YET POWERFUL LEARNING AND TEACHING TECHNIQUE	88
SPEED UP THESE CHORD CHANGES IN ONE MINUTE	89
F CHORD IS EASY BUT WHY IS IT SO HARD	91
A PRICELESS LEARNING AND TEACHING TECHNIQUE FOR BEGINNERS	93
MOON ROSE GUITAR PRACTICE PROGRAM WEEK TEN	94

WEEK ELEVEN   LESSON ELEVEN

THE ART OF FAST CHORD CHANGING	96
THE GOLDEN SECRET	97
IT'S SO SIMPLE EVERYBODY MISSED IT	97
HOW TO PERFECT IT	99
A SIMPLE LEARNING AND TEACHING TECHNIQUE THAT WILL HELP YOU PLAY THOUSANDS OF SONGS	99
DIFFICULT CHORD CHANGES MADE EASY	102
ANOTHER INVALUABLE LEARNING AND TEACHING TECHNIQUE	102
HOW TO PERFECT G TO C	102
HOW TO PERFECT G TO D	103
HOW TO PERFECT C TO D	104
MOON ROSE GUITAR PRACTICE PROGRAM WEEK ELEVEN	106

WEEK TWELVE   LESSON TWELVE

HOW TO PLAY SONGS	108
THIS SKILL IS IN ALL SONGS	112
A CHORD CHANGE EXPLAINED IN DETAIL	112
NOW YOUR GUITAR IS EASIER TO PLAY	113
NOW YOU HAVE IT ALL	116
GUITAR CHORDS BACK TO FRONT	117
THE BEST GUITAR CHORDS	119
BELIEVING IN YOURSELF	124
PROGRESS CHART	125
MOON ROSE GUITAR PRACTICE PROGRAM WEEK TWELVE	127

MOON ROSE

*GUITAR
LESSON ONE*

THE FOUR REASONS FOR FAILURE
AND HOW TO AVOID THEM

THE FOUR REASONS FOR FAILURE
AND HOW TO AVOID THEM

It is today, and always has been my experience that these are the reasons why so many thousands of people have failed to become good guitar players.
1. BAD THUMB POSITIONING BEHIND THE NECK.
2. NOT STRENGTHENING YOUR WEAKER THIRD, AND FOURTH FINGERS.
3. LEARNING G CHORD THE WRONG WAY
4. LEARNING RHYTHMS THE WRONG WAY

If you neglect these vital starting points it is impossible to become a good guitarist. That is why I am bringing it to your attention now. If, on the other hand you take the time to correctly develop these skills, you have just about written your own guarantee of success.

Every year I have people enrolling in our schools that have been taking lessons elsewhere, or teaching themselves without much success. If they were making progress they would not have to contact us in the first place. My focus with these people is not to teach them, but to find out what went wrong. The problems are always traced back to the four faults mentioned here. Once they are aware of this their progress is absolutely amazing.

It is very unfortunate that almost all failed guitarists would have succeeded had they been aware of this from the start. It is also very sad because it was not their fault. How could a beginner know this? It was mostly our fault as teachers and writers that they failed. When someone reaches out their hand to learn, it is our responsibility as guitar teachers to show them the right way from the very start. If you succeeded you were obviously with a good teacher, or had a good book.

Almost all books, videos, dvd's, learning from the internet, good players trying to teach guitar, are so focused on songs and chord fingering that they have forgotten completely to tell you that none of this is actually possible without the following; 1.Very good thumb positioning behind the neck of your guitar. 2. Strengthening your weaker third and fourth fingers. 3. Learning G chord the right way from the start. 4. Learning rhythms correctly from the start.
How do I know this? From meeting thousands of people from all over the world, who have tried methods, and a few more, and failed.

To succeed we need to show you how to play, not what to play. That should be your choice once you have mastered the fundamentals of good guitar playing.

If your thumb is not correctly positioned behind the neck at all times, it is impossible to finger most chords properly. It is also completely impossible to change quickly from one chord to the next, and thirdly your guitar will never sound good all the time.

If your third and fourth fingers are not developed correctly from the start they will not become independent of each other. Neither will you ever have four fingers to play guitar as professionals do. And thirdly you will never be able to stretch them properly to make barre chords, and power chords easy to play.

Learning G chord the wrong way from the start makes it very difficult to change to D and C quickly and easily. It also is impossible to include smooth bass runs and ornamentation.

If you have been learning guitar without addressing these issues, I urge you to do so from today. They are the same as building a house on a rock. It lasts a lifetime. Neglecting these skills as you learn is the same as building your house on quicksand. It does not last very long.

A good guitar teacher, or book will put you on the right road from the very start. As well as saving you a lot of time, money, and frustration, they will make sure that you avoid the pitfalls that are waiting for you should you neglect, 1 thumb positioning, 2, finger strengthening, 3, learning G chord the right way, and 4, good timing.

GETTING STARTED THE RIGHT WAY <u>OPENS DOORS</u> TO THE FUTURE
GETTING STARTED THE WRONG WAY <u>CLOSES DOORS</u> TO THE FUTURE

In this book I am showing you the best possible way to start learning guitar, if you want to become a good player. It is impossible to improve on it because all the skills are technically 100%. They are exactly as played by professional guitarists, and I have seen them help over ten thousand people to become good guitarists. With a sincere effort they will work for you too.

MOON ROSE

GUITAR
LESSON TWO

BEFORE YOU START PLAYING

WHAT IS A SONG ON GUITAR
AM I LEFT HANDED OF RIGHT HANDED
WHAT IS THE BEST KIND OF GUITAR TO LEARN ON
WHAT TO LOOK FOR WHEN BUYING A GUITAR
WHAT ELSE WILL I NEED
THE BEST PLECTRUM TO USE

WHAT IS A SONG ON GUITAR

Every song that ever was or will be played on guitar is actually a combination of just three things;

GOOD SOUND   GOOD TIMING   GOOD CHORD/NOTE CHANGES

- It makes no difference how old or new a song is
- It can be easy or difficult to play
- It can be any nationality or style
- It might be anything from Flamenco, Jazz, Metal, or Rock, to Classical Folk, or Traditional.
- It may be electric, acoustic, nylon string, twelve string, or any other style not mentioned.
- It does not matter whether you are playing guitar for twenty years or if its your first day.

At the end of the day it always comes back to good rhythm, clear sound, and good chord/note changing.

FOCUS POINT FOR STUDENTS AND TEACHERS

In the early weeks of learning guitar it is not realistic to instantly combine these three areas with any degree of success. A more clear minded and practical approach would be to improve each area individually as follows;

STEP 1   Your fretting hand   (five minutes)

STEP 2   Your rhythm hand   (five minutes)

STEP 3   Both hands together (five minutes)

This is a simple approach but it guarantees results. The right way to play guitar is also the easiest way once you have mastered the technique. By (1) practicing with one hand, (2) practicing with the other hand, and (3) only then playing with both hands together, you are certain to improve.

AM I LEFT HANDED OR RIGHT HANDED

The answer believe it or not is that when it comes to learning guitar there is no such thing as left handed, or right handed. It is an illusion. If you go to our pocket guitar you will see how it works both ways. When learning, and playing a guitar you have a fretting hand, and a rhythm hand.

When you are buying a guitar that is a different story. It is then that you need to know, which is your rhythm hand, and fretting hand. You do not want to start learning on a right handed guitar, only to find out a few months later that you should have been playing a left handed one. The easiest way to find out is to try both and see which is the most comfortable to strum. A good guitar teacher will quickly put you right also.

WHAT IS THE BEST TYPE OF GUITAR TO LEARN ON

Ideally a steel stringed six string acoustic guitar is best in the beginning. There are three very important reasons for this. Because of the sound quality, you, or a good teacher will have the opportunity to develop your listening skills while showing you how to play. It strengthens your fingers in order to produce pure sound. Because the fret board layout and neck size is the same as an electric guitar you will be able to learn electric, acoustic, and classical guitar from the beginning.

WHAT TO LOOK FOR WHEN BUYING A GUITAR

As I have just said the first thing to establish is if you need a right handed, or a left handed guitar. From that point on, to keep it simple you have a fretting hand, and a rhythm hand.

If you are in the process of buying a guitar be careful. You will very often be advised to buy a three quarter size, for under tens, or a nylon string if its for you and you are a beginner.

 The problem here is that you are being advised by a person who is probably very good as a sales assistant, but knows absolutely nothing about what you really need, in order to make your musical journey, as easy, productive, and enjoyable as possible.

The most important thing to get right when buying a guitar is the neck size. A full sized guitar with a slim neck is much easier to learn on, especially for children, or anyone with small hands, than a smaller size which usually has a wide neck. Most electric and acoustic guitars are now produced with slim necks. Professional guitarists use slim necked acoustic and electric guitars (except classical) so why not you. If you are a beginner my advice is to buy an acoustic guitar priced US $150 to $200.

WHAT ELSE WILL I NEED

If you are buying a guitar it is also a good idea to get a padded bag for two reasons: It will protect it from wear and tear when you are on the move. Also when you are not practicing put it back in the bag to keep the strings clean. Your strings will last up to ten times as long if you put it away after use. You will also need a capo (see picture) and a guitar tuner. It will take you up to six months to learn to tune by ear. In the beginning it is much easier and quicker to buy a guitar tuner which comes with a good instruction book. It will enable you to tune the strings almost instantly, or with the help of a friend, while you are waiting for your listening skills to develop.

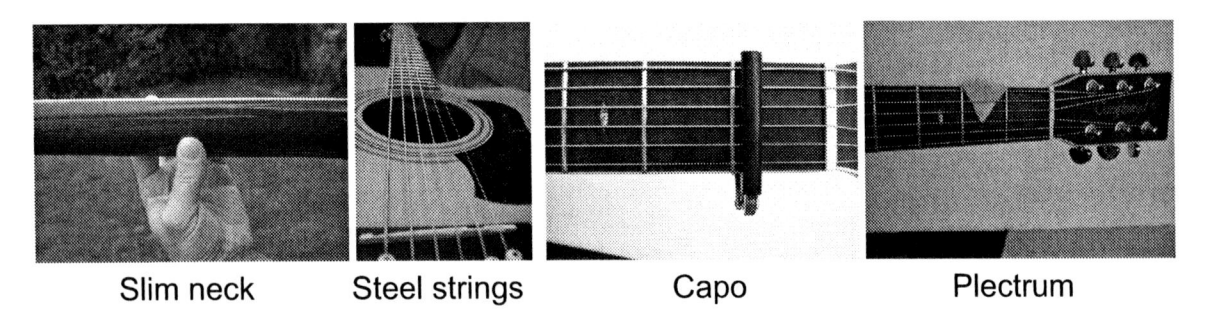

Slim neck   Steel strings   Capo   Plectrum

WHAT TYPE OF PLECTRUM SHOULD I USE

You may not believe this but you could be playing great guitar, putting all the right things in the right place at the right time, but sound bad. Why? **Because you have the wrong plectrum in your hand for the type of guitar you are playing.**

One of the best plectrums to use for playing acoustic guitar is the herdim plec in the picture. It is light enough not to slip too much in your hand especially when you are starting off. Because it is pointed you will find it much easier to pick individual strings when playing ornamentation and lead lines.

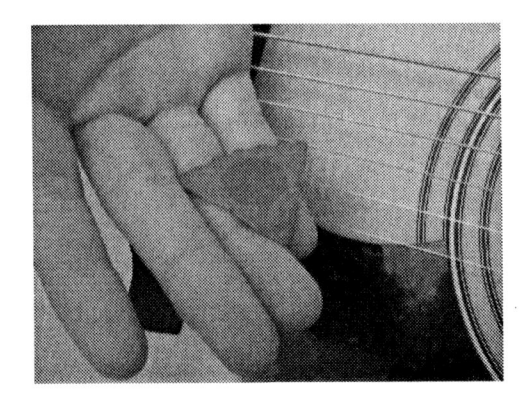

The pointed plectrum also gives off a much brighter sound when you strum, or pick an acoustic guitar, than a round tipped, or harder plectrum. Also when it wears you will be able to sharpen it with a nail file and it will be as good as new. However this plectrum is really not suitable for electric guitar.

For electric guitar you will need something harder because very often you will be digging the strings rather than strumming them. A three sided plectrum would be better again. When it slips you will be able to use one of the other sides and keep playing.

Every time you finish practicing, or playing it is a great idea to place your plectrum between the strings. It will always be there the next time you pick up your guitar. Place your plectrum on the guitar over the fifth fret. slide it over the sixth string, under the fifth string, and over the fourth string. Now slide it back to the second fret and see how secure it is. Isn't that a simple time and money saving idea.

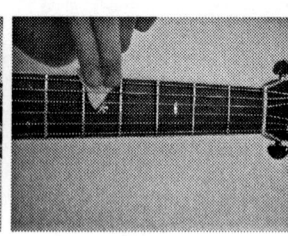

IF YOU DO THIS YOU WILL NEVER **LOSE** YOUR PLECTRUM
IF YOU DON'T DO THIS YOU WILL NEVER **FIND** YOUR PLECTRUM

MOON ROSE
GUITAR
LESSON THREE

TO HELP YOU GET STARTED

THE MOON ROSE POCKET GUITAR
(TO HELP YOU GET STARTED)
UNDERSTANDING THE FRETBOARD AND STRINGS
THE SIMPLE BUT ABSOLUTELY ESSENTIAL BASICS OF GREAT GUITAR PLAYING

THE
MOON ROSE
POCKET GUITAR ©

IMAGINATION IS MORE IMPORTANT THAN KNOWLEDGE

HERE IS A GUITAR
TO HELP YOU GET STARTED

Here is a little surprise and a wonderful learning aid if you have decided to start playing guitar, or do not have much time to practice. You will receive another much bigger surprise near the end of this book once you have become reasonably skilled on guitar.

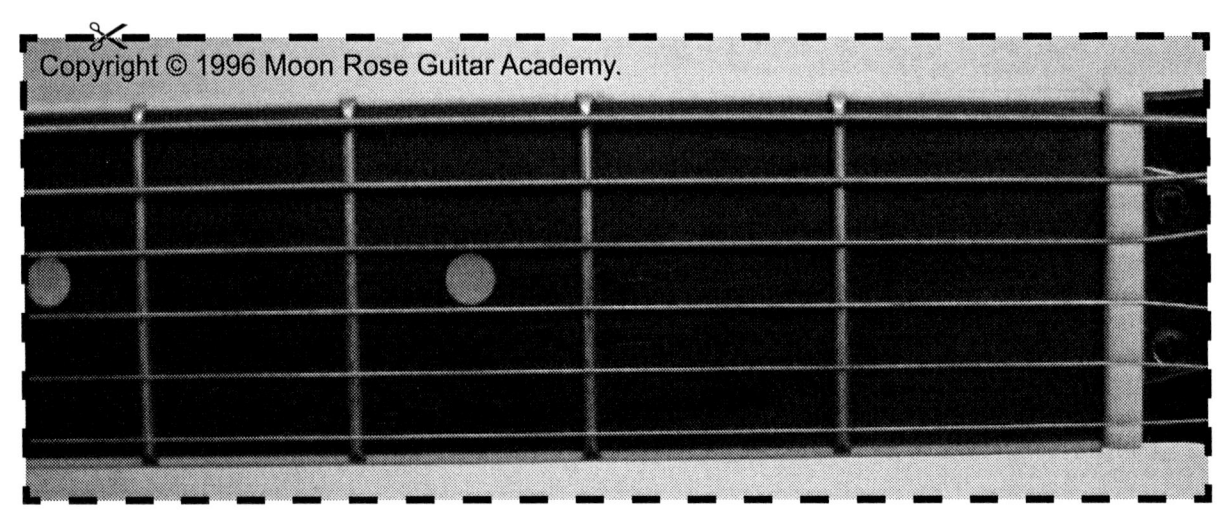

Copyright © 1996 Moon Rose Guitar Academy.

Cut out this guitar neck and stick it to a piece of wood approximately the same size. It does not have to be a perfect measurement as guitar necks vary in size, but it will help you get started and speed up your progress.

Much of my time with Moon Rose Guitar Academy is dedicated to finding ways of making it easier for people to improve once they start learning guitar. Here is an idea I came up with that cost nothing and yet proved invaluable to thousands of students as a learning aid. This simple idea saved time, especially for adults.

If you do not have a guitar to learn on, or find it difficult to bring one on your travels here is a simple practice aid that you can use anywhere, anyplace, anytime, and without disturbing anybody. Simply cut out one of the guitar necks like this one on the back page or back cover. It will fit in your pocket and can be used on trains, planes, or whenever you have some free time to perfect you newly acquired chords, skills, and techniques. It is also invaluable when your finger tips get sore. You will still be able to learn your chords on one of these without hurting your fingers.

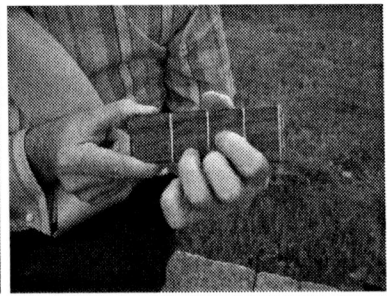

I invented it about nine years ago simply because our adult students did not have as much time to practice as the younger ones, and therefore progressed at a slower pace. Once we introduced the pocket guitar the results were absolutely amazing.

I have included it in this book for four very important reasons. First of all you or one of your friends may not have a guitar, but would like to start learning. If this is so you can make a copy and pass it on. They can attach it to a piece of wood and get started.

Secondly, you may not be able to practice much at home but could use it at different times during the day when you get a few minutes. Almost all the skills in this book can be perfected on the pocket guitar. It is a very simple, clear minded, and practical idea, and you can bring it anywhere with you.

Thirdly, everybody gets sore fingers in the early weeks of learning. When this happens you will be able to continue practicing on the pocket guitar without hurting your fingers. As well as being easier on your finger tips it also speeds up your progress.

Isn't it amazing that it can be used two ways? Earlier in this book I mentioned that left handed and right handed is just an illusion, and that we are all the same when it comes to learning guitar. Here again you will see how it makes no difference if you strum with your right hand, or left hand.

The
Moon Rose
Pocket Guitar

WORKS FOR BOTH
LEFT HANDED AND RIGHT HANDED GUITAR PLAYING.

RIGHT HANDED

LEFT HANDED

Stick it to a piece of timber approximately the same size. The piece of wood does not have to be very accurate as guitar necks vary slightly in size.

HOW TO USE IT

THE FRETTING HAND
Hold it in your fretting hand and by copying the pictures in this book you will be able to learn the names and finger positions of all the chords in this book. All good guitar players know these chords off by heart. If you even memorized one chord every day very soon you will know all the chords in this book. These chords are used in millions of songs, and by all the greatest artists the world has ever known.

THE RHYTHM HAND

Now hold the guitar neck in your fretting hand and hold a plectrum in your rhythm hand. You can now practice rhythm patterns on it with your rhythm hand. To get the best results put on cd's of your favourite songs and follow the instructions and practice techniques I have outlined in the rhythm section of this book. You will very quickly be able to strum along with your cd' as if you are playing a real guitar.

FOR GUITAR TEACHERS

If you are a fellow guitar teacher here is something that I want to share with you. I do workshops for people who have never played guitar, or never had a guitar. For them I put forty of these pocket guitars into a shopping bag. If they were full size guitars I would need a big trailer to carry them around. In these classes the pocket guitar is equally as productive as a full size guitar. It gives everyone the opportunity to participate, and see what is required before they buy a guitar or enroll on a course of lessons.

It may initially take a few hours to make these. I went to a hardware store and got the wooden blocks sawn to order. You could buy a few lengths of skirting board and saw them into four inch blocks. You can copy the picture of the pocket guitar as many times as you want and attach them to blocks of wood.

They have helped me greatly over the years with my guitar teaching and I know they will help you too.

UNDERSTANDING
THE FRETBOARD AND STRINGS

Picture of pocket guitar again

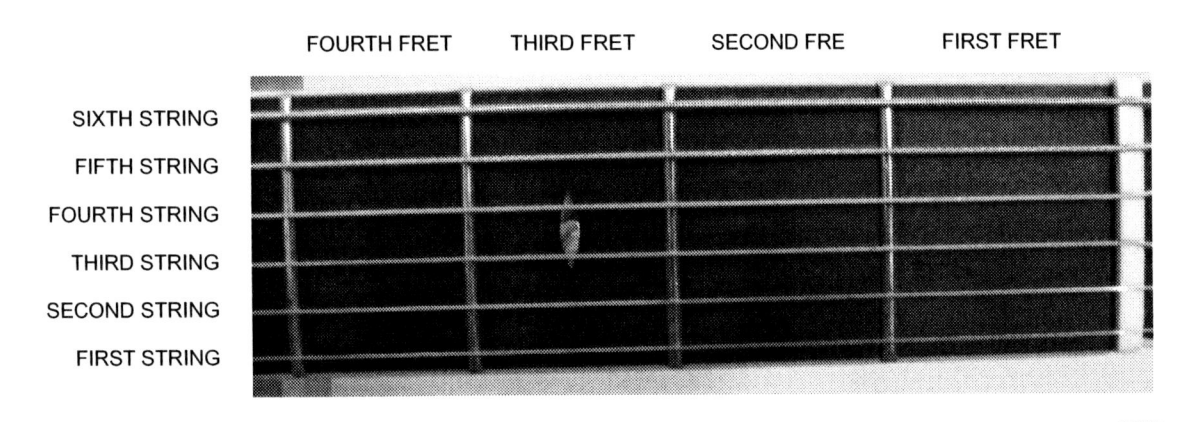

FOURTH FRET   THIRD FRET   SECOND FRE   FIRST FRET

SIXTH STRING
FIFTH STRING
FOURTH STRING
THIRD STRING
SECOND STRING
FIRST STRING

A CAPO
WHAT DO I NEED THAT FOR?

A capo is a guitar player's best friend. In the early days of learning it is impossible to appreciate how much a capo helps. The easiest explanation I can give you is that the guitar is always pitched to the vocalist in order to retain the quality of the voice. If the vocalist comes back to the guitar they lose their quality, and their audience. After all isn't it the words of our favorite songs that mean most to us, and then the guitar or music.

If you play a chord sequence on an open guitar it may suit your voice or it may not. If it does that's great. If it doesn't, you could try putting a capo on the second fret. The capo has now replaced the nut on your guitar which means that what was the third fret is now the first fret. Now all you have to do is play the same chord sequence again and the song is automatically pitched higher.

If this position suits your voice that's fine. If not you can move it up or down as many frets as you like until you find the position that is right for you. When you are putting a capo on the guitar it is important that you try to get it close to the fret maybe about a quarter of an inch back. In the picture the capo is in the ideal position. As you advance in your guitar playing you will see that the capo does a lot more than I have shown you here.

PRACTICE MAKES PERFECT.......RUBBISH.
PRACTICE DOES NOT MAKE PERFECT.

How many times have you heard this before? I have seen many students practice the wrong technique for hours and hours and get nowhere. In fact the more you practice faulty technique the worse you get. Then it is only a matter of time before you quit. PRACTICE DOES NOT MAKE PERFECT.

I have carefully laid out all the guitar lessons in this book and illustrated them as clearly as possible because I do not want this to happen to you. **Please read each lesson carefully** until you have a clear mental picture of how to practice. I have included a practice program for each lesson from here on for this and many other reasons. I can see what is ahead of you because I have been there thousands of times with people just like you.

By planning our practice we get a lot more done in a shorter space of time. The programmes break the different areas in smaller more manageable steps. They may not make much sense in the first two weeks but I promise you they get results.

WHAT GETS MEASURED GETS DONE

How true this is. From here on we have a planned course of action with one goal....... to become a good guitar player. To see how much you are improving we have laid out the lessons in weekly timeframes and included a progress chart. Fill this in at the end of each session. It may seem too simple to be of much benefit but it is the simple things that make us good guitarists.

Professionals have the patience to do simple things well. This gives them the ability to do difficult things easily. Isn't this a simple book so far? You need no knowledge of music whatsoever to learn from it. All the greatest artists the world has ever known had no knowledge of music whatsoever when they started. If they can do it, why not you?

As I said earlier "Before you practice please read each lesson carefully, and then practice carefully". If you practice each technique first slow, then medium, and eventually fast you are practicing perfectly. The biggest mistake of all is to move too fast with little attention to detail. If you tried to paint your bedroom in five minutes "what would it look like"? If you took your time and painted it with a lot of attention to detail "what would it look like?" Learning guitar is the very same.

PRACTICE DOES NOT MAKE PERFECT

PERFECT PRACTICE MAKES PERFECT

There is a big difference between these two approaches. Take your time and the skills you develop will last you a lifetime. If you can't play something slowly how can you play it fast? Everything I am showing you in this book is exactly as professionals play. I have not compromised once. Once you have mastered them they will last you for a lifetime.

MOON ROSE
GUITAR LESSON FOUR
(INTO ACTION)
YOUR FRETTING HAND

THE SIMPLE, BUT ESSENTIAL SKILLS OF
GREAT GUITAR PLAYING

GOOD POSTURE / GOOD SET UP / HOLDING YOUR GUITAR / THE INVISIBLE SKILL
ALL GREAT GUITAR PLAYING STARTS HERE
YOUR WEAK FINGERS (HOW TO STRENGTHEN THEM)
SOME OF THE INVISIBLE SKILLS OF GREAT GUITAR PLAYING
WHAT MANY TEACHING METHODS FORGET TO TELL YOU, BUT SHOULD
THE MOST IMPORTANT CHORD YOU WILL EVER LEARN ON GUITAR

THE SIMPLE, BUT ABSOLUTELY ESSENTIAL BASICS OF GREAT GUITAR PLAYING

POSTURE, SET UP, AND HOLDING YOUR GUITAR

It is always best to play from a sitting position until you can play your first song. The biggest danger to avoid is crouching, or bending over your guitar to see what you are trying to do. It is a very common problem all over the world among beginners, and professionals who started out with bad posture, and later was unable to change.

GOOD POSTURE   GOOD POSTURE   BAD POSTURE

If you develop a bad posture early on, it will be very difficult to correct later in life. It also makes it harder to sing, and if you play a lot, can, and probably will lead to lower back trouble when you get older. My teaching experience tells me that definitely in this area, prevention is better than cure. It is much better to have a good posture right from the start and once we are used to it, the guitar actually becomes much easier to play.

If you are already playing and find yourself leaning over a lot I urge you to change now. Instead of leaning forward to see what they are doing good guitarists tilt the guitar back slightly as in these pictures. By doing this they are able to sit tall and still see the strings. It will feel uncomfortable for a short time but I promise you that your musical adventure will be greatly enhanced by this simple change.

If you are a beginner you are the lucky one. You now have the opportunity to get this right from the very start, without feeling uncomfortable.

POSTURE CHECK

THE SIMPLE BUT ABSOLUTELY ESSENTIAL BASICS
OF GREAT GUITAR PLAYING

- **Sit tall** (Spine straight)
- **Head tilted slightly forward from your neck**
- **Guitar resting on your leg** (same as photo)
- **Top of guitar tilted back towards you until you can see all six strings on the fret board**

AN INVISIBLE SKILL

- Body of guitar tucked under the elbow of your rhythm hand. (This is very important). **This is the first of many invisible skills needed to play guitar well.** (See focus point below)
- **See if you can hold it under the elbow, and at the same time strum with your rhythm hand, without moving the guitar. (Your fretting hand should not be near the guitar when you are doing this.)**

FOCUS POINT FOR STUDENTS AND TEACHERS
AN INVISIBLE SKILL

BODY OF GUITAR TUCKED UNDER RHYTHM ARM

Before anybody plays a guitar it is well worth investing a little time in getting a set up, and posture that is comfortable, and is also suitable for playing.

Ignoring this makes learning unnecessarily more difficult. A good example is being able to hold the guitar under the elbow of your rhythm hand as mentioned above.

Many people who are playing for a while but are still having difficulty trying to master rhythms will now be able to trace it back to this skill.

By getting used to this starting position your guitar will now stay in one position, and you will also be strumming, or picking, from one position also.

If you have not focused on these simple basics before, I urge you to do so from here on. If you follow my instructions, and make a sincere effort, I guarantee that you will be more successful.

There are many, many people who are playing guitar for years and still cannot change quickly from one chord to the next. This can again be traced back to a faulty starting position. They are holding most of the weight of the neck in their fretting hand, which is making it almost impossible to change with any degree of success.

If this is you;

1. Hold the guitar as I suggested above, under the elbow of your rhythm hand.
2. Make sure that there is no weight whatsoever in the fretting hand.
    -1 Now when you fret a chord it will be much easier.

Also you will not have to hold the guitar when you are changing from one chord to the next.

ALL GREAT GUITAR PLAYING STARTS HERE

There are
three correct thumb positions
for
all songs on guitar

Here they are;

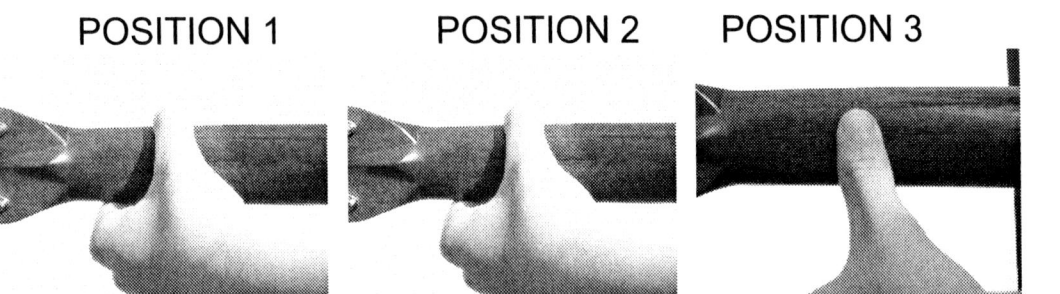

POSITION 1   POSITION 2   POSITION 3

EXAMPLE

OPEN CHORDS
THUMB TOUCHING SIXTH STRING

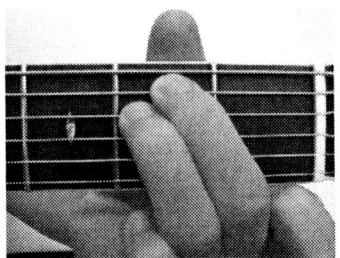

OPEN CHORDS
THUMB NOT TOUCHING SIXTH STRING

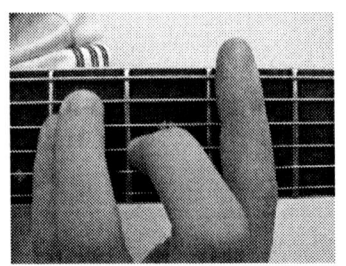

BARRE CHORDS
THUMB BEHIND NECK

To help you further with this hugely important step, when you are learning a chord or technique from a picture in this book, first copy the thumb position, and then copy the chord. Now your chances of success (even if you have failed before) are greatly increased. Because of this we have gone to great lengths to get the thumb positioning exactly right for you all through this book. If you are under twelve years of age, or have a small hand, you will not be able to reach the first position immediately. But do not worry. Time and some stretching will get you to the best position eventually.

> If you were asked to take just one thing from this book and nothing else, this is the skill I would recommend you take.
>
> WITHOUT YOUR THUMB **NOTHING** IS POSSIBLE
> WITH YOUR THUMB **EVERYTHING** IS POSSIBLE

It is almost impossible to fret many chords from these positions, and it is completely impossible to change quickly from one chord to another.

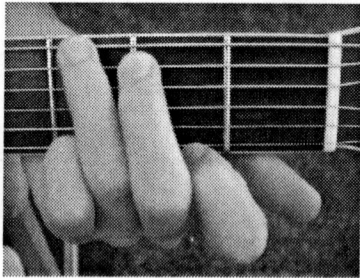

No   **No**   **No**

If you tried to learn before and found it difficult, or practically impossible to play, it is certain that you have neglected the importance of what happens behind the neck of the guitar. Here is a simple exercise that will instantly give you correct thumb positioning for all guitar songs. More importantly you will not have to relearn these skills later on. They are exactly the same for a professional as for a beginner, and easy to do. Correct thumb positioning opens the doors to great guitar playing, whereas faulty thumb positioning very quickly closes these doors.

MOON ROSE GUITAR
THUMB EXERCISE 1
THESE SKILLS WILL LAST A LIFETIME
THEY ARE IN EVERY SONG YOU WILL EVER PLAY ON GUITAR

1. Place your thumb on the neck of the guitar directly above the second fret. (Position 1)
   Your thumb is barely touching the sixth string to mute it.

2. Raise your thumb to position 2.
   Bend from your knuckle only.
   Now the sixth string will sound if you pick it.

3. Slide your thumb down to position 3.

4. Now slide your thumb back up to position 1.

5. Repeat the exercise five to ten times.

6. Now teach yourself a chord from this book as follows;
   (a) Copy the thumb position
   (b) Then, holding that thumb position, copy the finger positions.

That was a lot easier than you thought, wasn't it?

Take your fingers off the guitar and teach yourself the same chord again.

FOCUS POINT FOR STUDENTS AND TEACHERS

When someone decides to start playing guitar it is absolutely vital that the focus is on both the front, <u>and back</u> of the fret board right from the start.
One of the best ways to build this into your technique is to start learning chords from pictures as follows;
1. Copy the thumb position first.
2. Once you have done this then put your fingers on the fret board.
3. It will not work if you start with your fingers and then your thumb.

There is a big, big difference between the two.

If you are still not convinced
That your thumb is critical to good guitar playing
Try this

MOON ROSE GUITAR
THUMB EXERCISE 2

- Place your thumb behind the neck the same as this photograph

- Now place all your fingers on or close to the top string

- Now try to spread all four fingers across the top string only (without moving your thumb)

You cannot move them very far, can you? I am playing guitar since I was seven and I still cannot move my fingers when I try this.

- While holding your fingers on the top string can you now slide your thumb down, and behind the neck the same as this photograph.

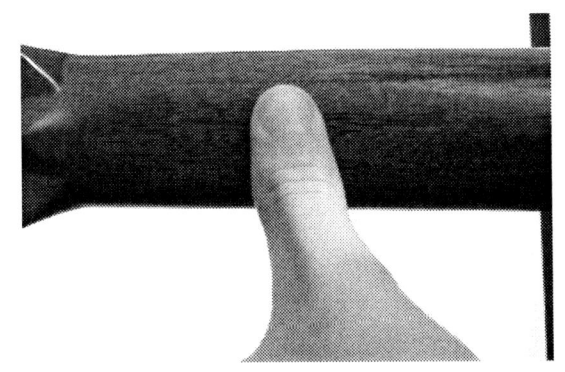

- Now try again to spread your fingers across the top string (while holding this thumb position)

- Now your fingers are finding it much easier to move across four, five , or even six frets.

I did not include this exercise just to show you how your thumb affects your fingers. It is also invaluable as a stretching exercise for your fingers and hand, and one of the starting positions on which almost all good guitar playing is based.

REASON TWO

YOUR WEAK FINGERS
AND
HOW TO STRENGTHEN THEM

If you tried to learn guitar before did this happened to you?

- You tried to move the second finger and the third one moved instead.
- You tried to move the third finger and maybe the first finger moved instead.

This is one of the most frustrating things to happen when you start learning guitar. We have to eliminate this, and quickly to help you to progress. As well as good thumb positioning all good players have four fingers capable of playing guitar. If you are a beginner, or are playing a few months you have only two, or if you are very lucky three fingers that are capable of fretting a guitar. If you do not believe me try this exercise. As well as eliminating this problem, and exposing all the weaknesses in your fretting hand, it is also the solution. It will give you many skills that are absolutely necessary for good guitar playing.

This exercise gives you sixteen skills that can be found in every song that ever was, or will be played on guitar. They are all used by the greatest artists the world has ever known, and is a great starting point for you too. Each time you practice this exercise, you narrow the gap between you and a professional guitarist. It is absolutely relevant to both acoustic, and electric guitar playing.

MOON ROSE GUITAR
FINGER EXERCISE 2
THESE SKILLS WILL LAST A LIFETIME

THEY ARE IN EVERY SONG
THAT EVER WAS OR WILL BE
PLAYED ON GUITAR

- Place your thumb centered behind the neck

- Then place your fingers across the top string, one in each fret, while at the same time maintaining the correct thumb position.

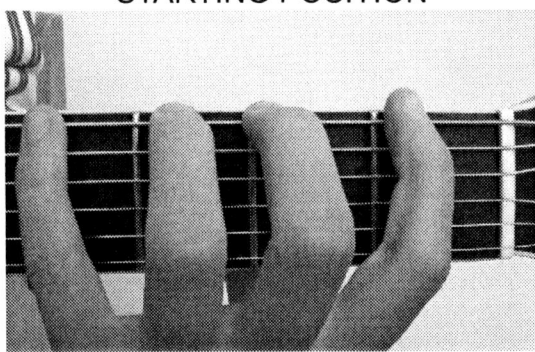

STARTING POSITION

- From here move your **first finger only** down to the fifth string, first fret.
- Now move your **second finger only** down to the fifth string, second fret.
- It is of vital importance that you are moving only one finger at a time, and also retaining the correct thumb position behind the neck.
- Now try to move your third finger down a string without moving the others. **Not so easy, is it.** Because it is still too weak to play guitar you can use your other hand to move it down. Don't worry about this. If you practice this exercise you will see a huge improvement in this finger in the next fifteen minutes.

Here is a full sequence of the exercise. At first you will be quite slow but you will speed it up within days.

STARTING POSITION

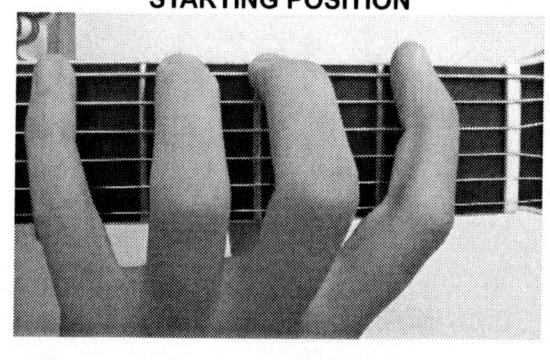

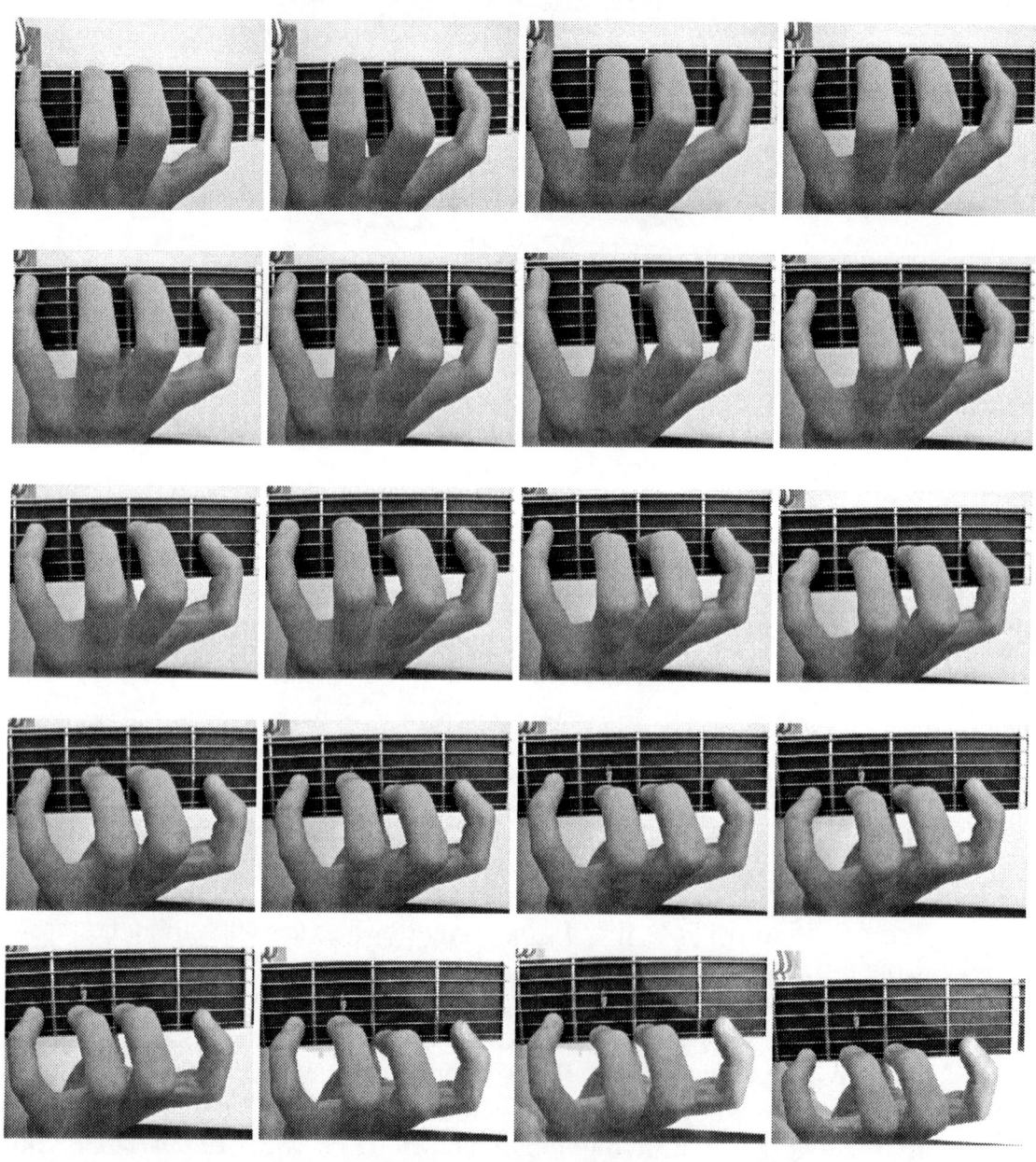

If you are feeling cramp during or after this exercise that is quite normal. Just rest your hand for a few minutes before starting again. Cramp is quite natural as we are exposing the weaknesses in your hand. But this is also the solution. In a weeks time you will be absolutely amazed at how much stronger your hand is, and how much easier it is to make your fingers go where you want them to go.

HOW DID I KNOW YOUR THIRD FINGER, AND MOST TIMES, YOUR LITTLE FINGER, WAS NOT STRONG ENOUGH TO PLAY GUITAR?

I have been asked this question at least ten thousand times and always will be, by anybody who wants to learn guitar. The answer is very simple. Just like a professional you need four fingers if you want to play good music. Before you start, or up to now in your life, you have really only used two. Think about it.

Each time you

Turn a key to open your front door

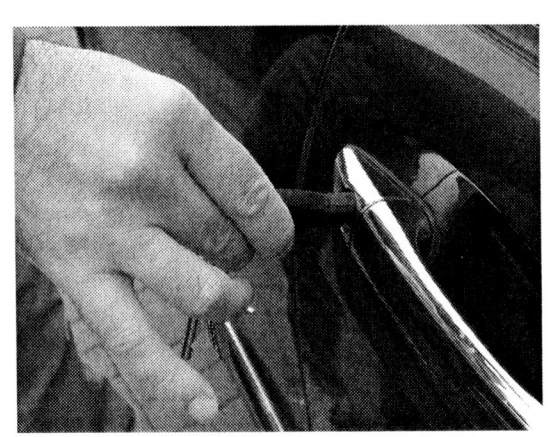

Turn a key to open a car

Use a knife, fork, or spoon

Hold a cup, mug, or glass

Use a mobile phone

Hold a golf ball, remote control, or some similar object
Write a letter
Use the mouse on a computer
Point at something

You use your first and second fingers as the power source. The list is endless. Can you look closely at these pictures, or try a few other general day to day hand movements yourself. Your third and little fingers are merely passengers. If you are a good typist or a pianist you are using all four fingers, but not with the strength that is required to play guitar.

This, like more learning techniques you will see later on is so obvious that almost all teachers and books overlook it. So you can see now I did not have to be a genius to know that you have only two fingers that are good enough to play guitar with today. You have been using them since you were born in everyday life, and the ones you were not using just need to be strengthened.

Even though this is just basic common sense, as are all my guitar classes,
It is yet again my personal experience that neglecting this and the thumb position are by far the top reasons why people fail to learn guitar.

If you neglect these two vital starting points it is impossible to become a good player. It is also **a guarantee of failure** when you try to advance. If, on the other hand you take the time to perfect these skills, you will find learning guitar much easier, and **your success is assured.**

FOCUS POINT FOR STUDENTS AND TEACHERS

One of the biggest mistakes we can make in the beginning is to focus on learning, songs without first looking at the thumb and fingering skills needed to play them well.

It is actually impossible to play a guitar without first learning, and being aware of these simple skills. They take only a few weeks to get good at, and make your life much easier, especially when you are ready to brighten your sound, and speed up your changes. The guitar cannot change to suit us, so we must mould both of our hands to suit the guitar.

These skills are also a key reason why good guitarists make songs look so easy whereas others who have been playing for years still make it look like hard work. They also eliminate unnecessary and waste movement right from the start.

TAKE YOUR TIME

So, whether you are teaching, or learning, please focus on both of these exercises. Take your time and get them right. They are invaluable. If you do not believe me turn on your tv some night, or the next time you are at a show, or concert, and watch the guitar players in the group. You will look at them from a different viewpoint.

Each time you practice you are closing the gap, and developing the skills you really need. More to the point you are working on skills that are manageable right now, and who knows I might be watching you on tv someday. You would not be the first one. Some of our past students, who are now top class and successful guitarists, had to start from here. It was the thumb, and finger exercises that opened the way.

They have also discovered that no matter how good they get, style of music they want to play, number of people they perform to, or how many million cd's they sell, they still have to rely on these thumb, and finger skills.

SOME OF THE INVISIBLE SKILLS
OF
GREAT GUITAR PLAYING

As well as giving you four fingers capable of playing guitar this exercise gives you all of the following skills which are invisible to the naked eye, and yet they are absolutely necessary if we are to play guitar well. Have you ever tried to learn from a video, dvd, or a friend, but what you played sounded completely different to them. It is because you have not yet mastered some of the invisible skills shown here. The better you get at these, the closer your guitar will sound to the musician, or song you are trying to copy, and the easier it is to perfect.

Each time you repeat the finger exercise you are improving all of the following areas;

1. Strengthening the weaker third and/or fourth finger.
2. Making each finger completely independent of each other.
3. Develops correct thumb positioning behind the guitar.
4. Stretches your fingers to exactly what is required to play well.
5. Builds the power in your fingers that you will need for more advanced technique.
6. Make each finger go where you want it to go.
7. Builds accuracy in your fingertips, preparing you for lead guitar.
8. Develops the correct muscles *(music muscles)* in your hand, wrist and arm. The first few times you do this exercise you will feel some cramp set in, and this is a key reason why you may have problems when you try to play a fast song. Again if you keep doing the exercise, and give time time, speed playing should not be a problem later on.

These are just eight skills that will greatly improve your guitar playing, and they are all being developed at the same time. This will help you to see improvement quickly. There are actually many more skills being ingrained in your fretting hand but I have not mentioned them here to avoid confusion.

Believe it or not, all these skills are in all guitar songs, both electric, and acoustic. They always will be. Because the guitar cannot be changed to suit us, we have to mould the skills into our fingers, hands, and arms to suit it. Only then will we be able to go back and look at most of the books we already have or songs you may have downloaded and be able learn them.

I can promise you that the more, and faster you practice this exercise, the better you become as a guitar player when the skills are transmitted into your songs and music. I can also promise you that they are a absolutely necessary for good guitar playing wherever you are, and whatever music you wish to play.

WHAT MANY TEACHING METHODS FORGET TO TELL YOU, BUT SHOULD

(BRIDGING THE GAP)

All the fingering and thumb techniques described in this chapter are necessary if you are to successfully learn songs from any book, dvd, the internet or video that you might have.

Having worked successfully with thousands of guitar students, if you are a beginner, I can tell you that your two biggest hurdles are going to be

1. **Developing fast, clean, accurate chord changes, and**

2. **Developing clear and pure sound.**

If that is so, we guitar teachers, and writers should be concentrating a considerable amount of our effort in helping the new student overcome these difficult stages of learning.

If you make a sincere effort, and follow the practice tips, and programme, you will succeed. It has been my experience that after ten to twelve weeks of quality learning you will be able to refer back to your books, dvd's etc, which initially you could not follow. You will now see them in a very different light. Once you have good fingers, good sound, and fast changes, almost all the other books that you might have will prove very beneficial.

THE MOST IMPORTANT CHORD YOU WILL EVER LEARN ON GUITAR

E m
(The word minor in music means a sad sound)

AND
EVERYTHING YOU NEED TO KNOW ABOUT IT

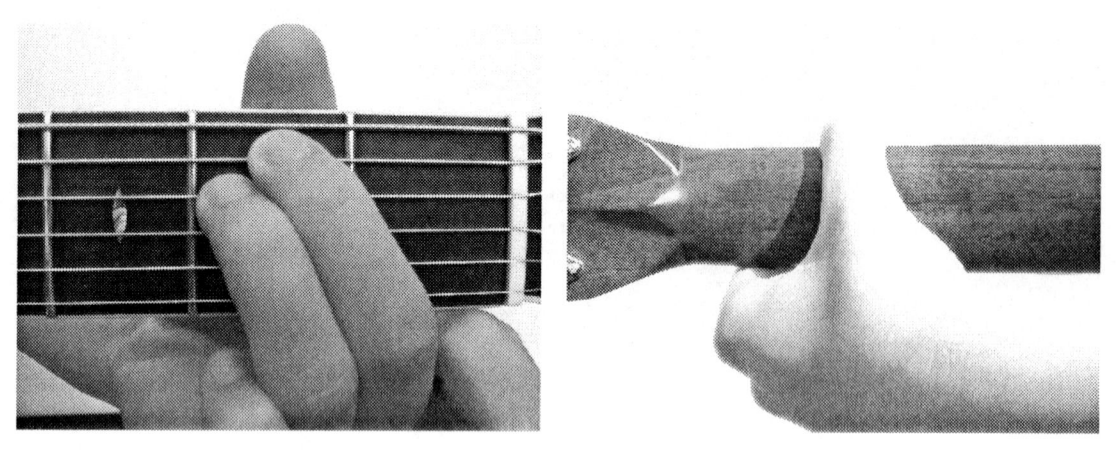

FRONT   BACK

THUMB DOES NOT TOUCH SIXTH STRING

LET US START BY FORMING TWO REALLY GOOD LEARNING TECHNIQUES.
1, COPYING PICTURE CHORDS CORRECTLY
2, MEMORISING THE CHORDS

- **Position your thumb on top over the second fret.**

    It is not touching the sixth string.

- **Place your second finger on the fifth string, second fret.**

- **Add your third finger on the fourth string, second fret.**

- **Look at your fingers and say to yourself, or in your mind,** E minor

- **Take your fingers off the guitar.**

- **Start again, first with your thumb, then the fingers, and then say** E minor **to help memorize the chord.**

Keep repeating this sequence until you can find the chord without having to look at the picture.

Please do not go to the next chord until you can do this one without looking at the picture.

MOON ROSE

GUITAR
PRACTICE PROGRAM
LESSON FOUR

ACHIEVEMENT IS SUCCESSFUL ACTION

1. CHECK YOUR SET UP   (GUITAR SLIGHTLY TILTED BACK TO YOU).

2. POSTURE CHECK   (SIT TALL, HEAD UP, STRAIGHT BACK).

3. TUCK THE GUITAR UNDER YOUR STRUMMING ARM.

4. THUMB EXERCISE 1   FIVE TIMES.

5. THUMB EXERCISE 2   FIVE TIMES

6. FINGER EXERCISE 1   AT LEAST TWICE EACH DAY. IF YOU GET INTO
                               DIFFICULTY IT JUST MEANS THAT YOUR THUMB HAS
                               SLIPPED OUT OF POSITION BEHIND THE NECK.

7. READ THE SECTION "GETTING STARTED THE RIGHT WAY" A FEW TIMES TO GIVE YOURSELF A CLEAR MENTAL PICTURE OF WHERE YOU ARE GOING.

8. PRACTICE Em CHORD.   KEEP REPEATING IT UNTIL YOU CAN DO IT WITHOUT
                               THE BOOK. IT ONLY TAKES A FEW MINUTES AND IS THE
                               MOST IMPORTANT CHORD YOU WILL EVER LEARN ON
                               GUITAR.FINISH YOUR PRACTICE BY PLACING THE
                               PLECTRUM BACK BETWEEN THE STRINGS. IT WILL BE
                               THERE THE NEXT TIME YOU PICK UP YOUR GUITAR.

9. FINALLY FILL IN YOUR PROGRESS CHART AT THE BACK OF THIS BOOK.

MOON ROSE

GUITAR LESSON FIVE

YOUR RHYTHM HAND

THE BEST WAY TO STRUM A GUITAR
A SIMPLE, BUT AMAZING PRACTICE TECHNIQUE
START DEVELOPING YOUR LISTENING SKILL NOW

YOUR RHYTHM HAND

This is probably hard for you to believe but all songs strummed on guitar are actually played using just one foundation rhythm. I will prove this to you later on, and you can then turn on your tv , or go to a gig to watch a guitarist, if you want even more proof.

Here lies one of the great differences between professionals, and amateurs. Because I want you to become a good guitarist and because it is so important to start the right way I am pointing this out to you now. It is yet again one of the optical illusions of great guitar playing. Our head will tell us that different rhythms must mean different patterns with our rhythm hand, when in reality most of the rhythm changes are actually initiated by your fretting hand.

THE PROFESSIONAL APPROACH

The best way to get good at something is to have the same approach; rhythm after rhythm, night after night, year after year. Very quickly it becomes simple, and easy to repeat. This is why professionals are so good. They have only one way of playing guitar (THE RIGHT WAY), and do the same thing song after song, night after night. The professional approach is fully explained in lesson seven.

THE AMATEUR APPROACH

I have met many guitarists who had not realized their potential. One of the things that held them all back was the way they approached rhythms. They tried to learn hundreds of them in hundreds of different ways.

I was very fortunate to have one of the great guitarists sit with me and reveal the importance of a professional approach right from the beginning. He had nine world tours behind him at that time so it is not to be taken lightly.

We are going to introduce you to good timing with a very simple step, but I can assure you that it is totally in keeping with professional guitar playing, as is every lesson, tip, and learning technique in this book.

THE BEST WAY TO STRUM A GUITAR

if you are just starting is to

1. Strike six strings for all downstrokes, and up strokes and

2. It is also important that you strum from over the centre of the sound hole.

A SIMPLE BUT AMAZING PRACTICE TECHNIQUE

Can you hold your guitar, tucked under your arm, and sit comfortably just like I am doing in the picture. Then vamp all six strings with your fretting hand. If you are doing this correctly you can now strum with a plectrum across the strings and all you will hear is a flat or vamped sound.

WEIGHT OF THE GUITAR
UNDER YOUR ARM

VAMP STRINGS
NO SOUND WHEN YOU STRUM

MOON ROSE GUITAR
RHYTHM EXERCISE 1

- Body of guitar tucked under your strumming arm.
- Tap your foot as if you were listening to a slow song
- In your mind, or out loud, count 1, 2, 3, 4, 1, 2, 3, 4, 1, 2, 3, 4,
- Keep counting and with a plectrum start strumming your guitar at the same time (using downstrokes only).
- Make sure that the downstrokes are sounding the strings at exactly the same time as you are saying each number.
- If you are doing this correctly your rhythm hand will be going down, and hitting the strings, as your foot is going down. It will be coming back up (but not hitting the strings) as your foot is coming back up.

- Then try this with your thumb and first finger instead of a plectrum. If you are doing it correctly your thumb will strum downstrokes and your first finger will strum the upstrokes.

As you get better at this practice technique you can start speeding it up. All songs played on guitar can be traced back to this simple learning technique. It is done slowly in slow songs, and fast in fast songs. The better you get at this, and it does not take long, the easier it will be for you to learn more difficult rhythms later on.

Even though this technique is vital to all future rhythms, it is very easy to practice because you are focused on one hand only. It is a very manageable step, and also great fun if you can do it along with a cd.

> **Now stop reading this book for five minutes and practice the strumming exercise.**

FIVE MINUTES LATER
That was easier than you thought. Wasn't it.
Now we can take it a step further and make it much more fun.

START DEVELOPING YOUR LISTENING SKILLS NOW

A lot of guitarists play with their hands. It is not enough.
   All great musicians play with
   1. their hands,
   2. their ears, and
   3. their imagination.

I can tell you from my own personal experience that it will greatly enhance your musical journey if I can get you to develop not just finger skills, but also your listening skills at the same time. This is the starting point which in time will give you the ability to recognize musical sounds instantly (playing by ear).

PRACTICING THIS EXERCISE WITH A CD.

Assuming that you can now strum slowly can you put on a cd of any slow song, but ideally one that you like, and follow these steps;
- As the song is playing tap your foot to the beat
- Try to sense out 1, 2, 3, 4, 1, 2, 3, 4,
- Strum your guitar along with the cd
- If you can't get the beat stop, and start again. Each time you try it gets easier.
- Why is this exercise harder to play with a cd, than on your own. Because we now have to play with our ears as well as our hands. We have to

listen to the beat in order to stay on time, a crucial skill if you are to become a good guitarist.

If you have been playing for a while but still cannot play with other musicians this will also help you to overcome that problem.

FOCUS POINT FOR STUDENTS AND TEACHERS

When teaching, or learning guitar rhythms, it makes much more sense to develop both finger skills, and listening skills from the very start. People who play guitar with their hands only do not get very far.

One of the many invisible skills of the great guitar players is their ability to listen and play at the same time. On that basis if we are going to be professional in our approach to teaching, and learning guitar we need to work on both areas as quickly as possible. This is not difficult. The learning and practice techniques here are guaranteed to get you started the right way.

MOON ROSE
GUITAR PRACTICE PROGRAM
LESSON FIVE

> FAILURE CANNOT COPE WITH PERSISTENCE

1. **CHECK YOUR SET UP** — (GUITAR SLIGHTLY TILTED BACK TO YOU).

2. **POSTURE CHECK** — (SIT TALL, HEAD UP, STRAIGHT BACK). TUCK THE GUITAR UNDER YOUR STRUMMING ARM.

3. **THUMB EXERCISE 1** — FIVE TIMES.

4. **THUMB EXERCISE 2** — FIVE TIMES

5. **FINGER EXERCISE 1** — AT LEAST TWICE EACH DAY. IF YOU GET INTO DIFFICULTY IT JUST MEANS THAT YOUR THUMB HAS SLIPPED OUT OF POSITION BEHIND THE NECK.

6. READ THE SECTION "GETTING STARTED THE RIGHT WAY" A FEW TIMES TO GIVE YOURSELF A CLEAR MENTAL PICTURE OF WHERE YOU ARE GOING.

7. **PRACTICE Em CHORD.** — KEEP REPEATING IT UNTIL YOU CAN DO IT WITHOUT THE BOOK. IT ONLY TAKES A FEW MINUTES AND IS THE MOST IMPORTANT CHORD YOU WILL EVER LEARN ON GUITAR.

8. **PRACTICE STRUMMING** — PLAY FROM THE MIDDLE OF THE SOUND HOLE AND STRUM SIX STRINGS FOR ALL DOWNSTROKES, AND UP STROKES.

9. **RHYTHM EXERCISE 1** — PRACTICE STRUMMING. MAKE SURE THE STRINGS ARE VAMPED WITH YOUR FRETTING HAND. NOT ONLY ARE YOU NOT UNDER PRESSURE TO PLAY THE RIGHT CHORDS, BUT ALSO YOU CAN ACTUALLY STRUM YOUR GUITAR TO YOUR FAVOURITE CD'S.

10. **PLAY Em** — WITH YOUR FRETTING HAND, AND STRUM THE GUITAR WITH YOUR RIGHT HAND.

11. FINISH YOUR PRACTICE BY PLACING THE PLECTRUM BACK BETWEEN THE STRINGS. IT WILL BE THERE THE NEXT TIME YOU PICK UP YOUR GUITAR.

12. FINALLY FILL IN YOUR PROGRESS CHART AT THE BACK OF THIS BOOK.

BECAUSE YOUR FINGERTIPS ARE PROBABLY SORE, AND NOT YET HARDENED, IT MAY NOT SOUND GREAT. IF YOU STICK WITH IT AND MAKE A SINCERE COMMITMENT TO PRACTICE YOU ARE NOW ON THE ROAD THAT EVENTUALLY LEADS TO GREAT GUITAR PLAYING.

EACH TIME YOU COMPLETE THIS PROGRAMME YOU HAVE NARROWED THE GAP BETWEEN YOU AND A PROFESSIONAL GUITARIST.

MOON ROSE
GUITAR LESSON SIX

THE BEST WAY
TO LEARN GUITAR CHORDS

BUILDING A FOUNDATION TO GREAT GUITAR PLAYING
GUITAR SKILLS THAT LAST A LIFETIME
WHAT IS
E MINOR, MAJOR, M7, MAJ7, 7, SUS4,
WHAT DO THEY MEAN?
THE NEXT THREE MOST IMPORTANT CHORDS ON GUITAR
AND EVERYTHING YOU NEED TO KNOW ABOUT THEM

THE BEST WAY TO LEARN GUITAR CHORDS

NO CHORDS…………….…...NO SONGS
KNOW CHORDS………...KNOW SONGS

BUILDING A FOUNDATION TO GREAT GUITAR PLAYING

There are many ways to learn and teach guitar chords. Some methods are easy, some difficult, and some completely impossible. This is one of the key areas where real quality teaching and learning stands out.

The best way to do this is to get everything technically right from the very start.

> Just like building a house, the foundation is crucial. If you get it right you have something that will last a lifetime. Get it wrong and it falls apart. A good foundation to great guitar playing is accomplished by

1. Always positioning your thumb correctly before learning the chord.
2. **Correctly** learning the most important chords first
3. Learning these chords in a way that will make it easier to change from one to another
4. Developing good sound at the same time.
5. Learning how to **correctly** teach yourself any chord you want

If you carefully follow the tips and practice techniques in the next few pages I can promise you that it is the best, and most professional way possible to start learning chords with your fretting hand.

GUITAR SKILLS
THAT WILL
LAST A LIFETIME

Have you ever been to a party or session and requested the guitarist to play one of your favorite songs on guitar.

Is this what happened;
GUITARIST A
He or she played the song and it was instantly recognizable. You would swear you were listening to the original version. It sounded beautiful and the guitarist made it look effortless, and easy to play.

Or

Is this what happened;
GUITARIST B
He or she played the song but it sounded the same as all the previous songs they played. There was a heavy hum, or booming sound from the guitar. There were no hooks, or recognizable fills, as everything was strummed. Their fretting fingers were all over the place, causing them to make faces, or even groan when trying the more difficult chord changes. They were hunched over the guitar.

If you are learning to play your goal should be to become GUITARIST A. You are already on the right road if you are learning from this book but it is crucial that you try to get the next few stages right. If you neglect the thumb position or the two finger exercise coming up the best you can hope for is something similar to GUITARIST B.

To help you over the next few hurdles I have included a daily planned practice programme, practice tips, and a progress chart at the back of this book. I urge you to stay with this for eight to twelve weeks. You will be amazed before you are half way through. Every day that you practice this way you are a step closer to success, and will be developing guitar skills that will last a lifetime.

WHAT IS
E MINOR, MAJOR, M7, MAJ7, 7, SUS4, WHAT DO THEY MEAN?

Here is a very simple explanation and really everything you need to know.

Minor
In music means a **sad** sound.

Example; Em Dm Bm Am. Any letter followed by a small m is a sad sounding chord.

Major

In music means a happy or lively sound.

It also means a complete or full sound.

Example

E   D   B   A   C   F

E is really E major. D is really D major, and C is really C major, etc.
Because it is automatically assumed that these are major chords the word major is not actually printed after them.

7

in music means a blues type sound.

Example

E7   D7   B7   A7

Any letter followed by the number 7 is a bluesy sounding chord as in twelve bar blues, but also used in many songs.

Minor7

in music means a sad bluesy sound.

Example

Em7   Dm7   Bm7   Am7

Any letter followed by a small m and the number 7 is a sad bluesy sounding chord.

Major7

In music means a | soft jazz | sound.

Example

Cmaj7   Dmaj7   Fmaj7   Amaj7

Any letter followed by maj7 is a soft jazz sounding chord. It is not confined to jazz music. It can be found in many songs, especially slow rock ballads.

SUS4

In music means an | incomplete | sound.
It also means a suspending, or in other words, a sound that is left up in the air.
To bring it down you have to play the major variation of the same chord directly afterwards.

Example

Csus4   Dsus4   Asus4   Gsus4

Any letter followed by sus4 is an incomplete sounding chord.

THE NEXT THREE MOST IMPORTANT CHORDS ON GUITAR

And everything you need to know about them

The next three chords to learn on guitar are Em7, D, Dsus4. For beginners these chords will not sound pure instantly. It takes about four to five weeks from when you first start playing to develop a reasonable sound, so don't be too impatient, or hard on yourself. Your priority right now is to learn the finger positions. It is only possible to develop good sound once you have achieved this. I have not written about sound for you yet because I would be wasting your time. You have to trust me on this. If you are with me so far, everything is unfolding perfectly, AND THE DAYS QUICKLY TURN TO WEEKS, TO MONTHS, TO YEARS.

For beginners it is impossible to appreciate the importance of the first seven chords in this book, but if you need confirmation ask any professional guitarist and they will verify this. It is my personal experience as a guitar teacher that all students look back after six months and then see clearly how vital it is to know these chords, and how to change from one to the other quickly, and easily.

The word minor in music means a sad sound, and major chords such as D, C, and G have happy sounds. As a musician when you say G, or E, or F, it is automatically assumed that you mean G major, E major, etc. You do not say "major". On the other hand if you are referring to any other type of chord you such as E minor, (SAD SOUND), D7 (BLUESY SOUND), Cmaj7, (SOFT JAZZ SOUND) must say it.

This is a very simple explanation and really all you need to know. If you think about it almost all songs are either happy, or sad. Therefore all minor chords are sad sounding, and all major chords such as D, C, and G, are happy, or lively sounding chords when they are strummed.

You may have heard the line of a famous song which went
 "How strange the change from major to minor", (from happy to sad).

Em7

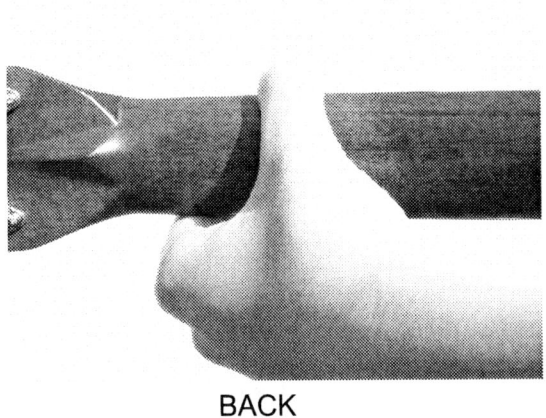

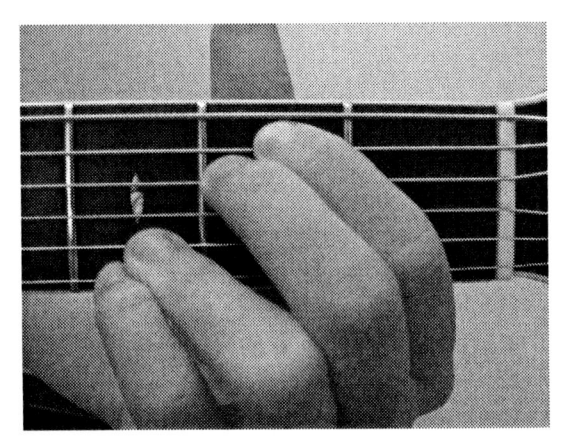

BACK　　　　　　　　　　　　　FRONT

THUMB DOES NOT TOUCH SIXTH STRING

- **Position your thumb on top over the second fret.**
  It is not touching the sixth string.

- **Place your first finger on the fifth string, second fret.**

- **Add your second finger on the fourth string, second fret.**

- **Add your third finger on the second string, third fret.**

- **Look at your fingers and say to yourself, or in your mind,**

  | E minor 7 |

- **Take your fingers off the guitar.**

- **Start again, first with your thumb, then the fingers, and then**

  say | E minor 7 | to help memorize the chord.

Keep repeating this sequence until you can find the chord without having to look at the picture.

Please do not go to the next chord until you can do this one without looking at the picture.

D

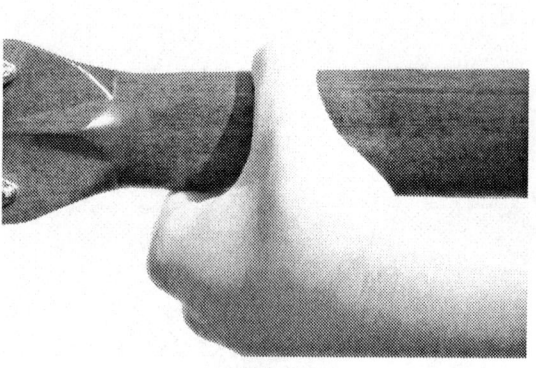

BACK    FRONT

THUMB TOUCHES SIXTH STRING

- **Position your thumb on top over the second fret.**
It is touching the sixth string.

- **Place your first finger on the third string, second fret.**

- **Place your second finger on the first string, second fret.**

- **Place your third finger on the second string, third fret.**

- **Look at your fingers and say to yourself, or in your mind,**
  boxed: D

- **Take your fingers off the guitar.**

- **Start again, first with your thumb, then the fingers, and then** say
  boxed: D **to help memorize the chord.**

Keep repeating this sequence until you can find the chord without having to look at the picture.

Please do not go to the next chord until you can do this one without looking at the picture.

D sus4

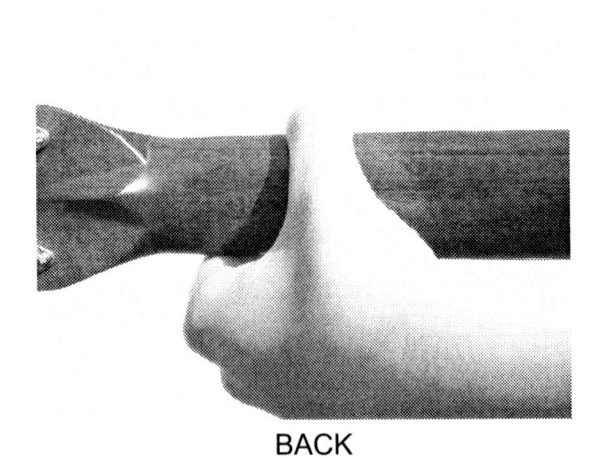

BACK   FRONT

THUMB TOUCHES SIXTH STRING

Here is a very quick way to learn this chord.
If you have learned D correctly all you have to do is
- Add your fourth (little) finger on the first string, third fret, to a D chord, and you now have Dsus4.
- Now take off your little finger. You are back to D chord.
- Add the little finger. You now have Dsus4 again.

Sometimes Dsus4 can be played with your second finger off the guitar as in the picture. It is your choice which way you want to play and it does not affect the sound.

Keep repeating this sequence until you can find both chords without having to look at the picture.

MOON ROSE

GUITAR
PRACTICE PROGRAM
MOON ROSE
LESSON SIX

SIMPLICITY AND SUCCESS ARE SYNONYMOUS

1. CHECK YOUR SET UP — GUITAR SLIGHTLY TILTED BACK TO YOU

2. POSTURE CHECK — SIT TALL, HEAD UP, STRAIGHT BACK.

3. THUMB EXERCISE 1 — FIVE TIMES.

4. THUMB EXERCISE 2 — FIVE TIMES.

5. — TUCK GUITAR UNDER STRUMMING ARM.

6. FINGER EXERCISE 1 — AT LEAST TWICE EACH DAY. IF IT IS GETTING EASIER TO DO YOU WILL PROGRESS MORE FROM HERE ONWARDS BY;
   1. PRESSING HARDER WITH YOUR FINGERS, AND
   2. SPEEDING IT UP SLIGHTLY.

7. PRACTICE STRUMMING EXERCISE. — PLAY FROM THE MIDDLE OF THE SOUND HOLE AND STRUM SIX STRINGS FOR ALL DOWNSTROKES, AND UP STROKES.

8. PRACTICE EM, D, AND D SUS4 CHORDS — UNTIL YOU CAN DO THEM WITHOUT HAVING TO LOOK IN THE BOOK.

9. RHYTHM EXERCISE 1 — PRACTICE STRUMMING. MAKE SURE THE STRINGS ARE VAMPED WITH YOUR FRETTING HAND. STRUM FIRST OF ALL ON YOUR OWN, AND THEN TO YOUR FAVOURITE CD'S.

10. PLAY Em, D AND D SUS4 — WITH YOUR FRETTING HAND, AND STRUM THE GUITAR. IS IT TUCKED UNDER YOUR ARM? D, AND D SUS4 MAY NOT SOUND GREAT BUT DO NOT WORRY. THINK BACK TO WHEN YOU FIRST OPENED THIS BOOK. IF YOU ARE THIS FAR YOU HAVE COME A LONG WAY.

11. PLACE PLEC BACK BETWEEN THE STRINGS WHEN YOU FINISH.

12. FILL IN YOUR PROGRESS CHART.

I HAVE PLANNED THIS PRACTICE PROGRAMME TO GIVE YOU MAXIMUM IMPROVEMENT IN MINIMUM TIME. THE REASON WE ARE IMPROVING IS THAT WE ARE WORKING ON EACH AREA INDIVIDUALLY. THIS GUARANTEES MUCH HIGHER QUALITY WHEN WE FINALLY PUT IT ALL TOGETHER.

EVERY TIME YOU REPEAT THIS PROGRAMME YOU ARE A DAY CLOSER TO SUCCESS.

MOON ROSE

GUITAR
LESSON SEVEN

THE NEXT THREE
MOST IMPORTANT CHORDS
ON GUITAR

THE NEXT THREE MOST IMPORTANT CHORDS ON GUITAR
And everything you need to know about them

C

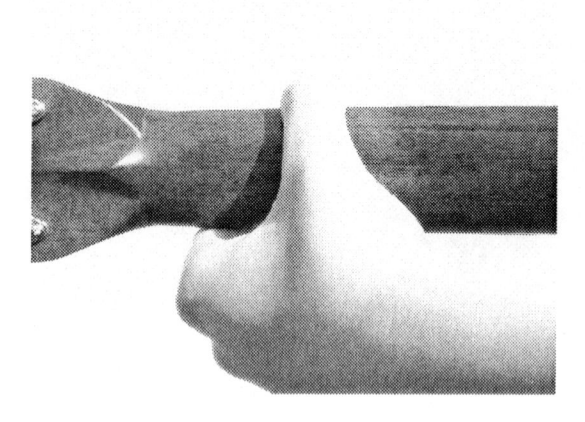

BACK 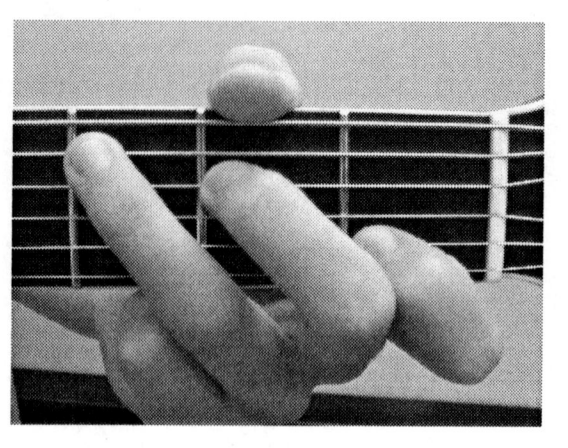　　　　　　　　　　　　FRONT

THUMB TOUCHES SIXTH STRING

- **Position your thumb on top over the second fret.**
  It is touching the sixth string.

- **Place your first finger on the second string, first fret.**

- **Add your second finger on the fourth string, second fret.**

- **Add your third finger on the fifth string, third fret.**

- **Look at your fingers and say to yourself, or in your mind, C.**

- **Take your fingers off the guitar.**

- **Start again, first with your thumb, then the fingers, and then say C to help memorize the chord.**

Keep repeating this sequence until you can find the chord without having to look at this page.

Please do not go to the next chord until you can do this one without looking at the picture.

C add9

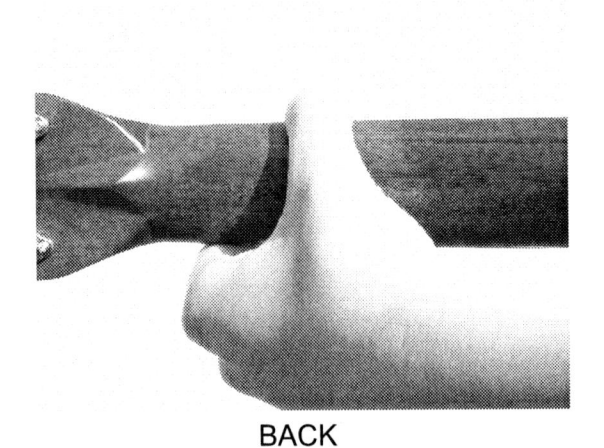

BACK 　　　　　　　　　FRONT

THUMB TOUCHES SIXTH STRING

- **Position your thumb on top over the second fret.**
  It is touching the sixth string.

- **Place your first finger on the fourth string, second fret.**

- **Place your second finger on the fifth string, third fret.**

- **Place your third finger on the second string, third fret.**

- **Look at your fingers and say to yourself, or in your mind,**

  | Cadd9 |

- **Take your fingers off the guitar.**

- **Start again, first with your thumb, then the fingers, and then
  say** | Cadd9 | **to help memorize the chord.**

Keep repeating this sequence until you can find the chord without having to look at the picture.

Please do not go to the next chord until you can do this one without looking at the picture.

Sometimes Cadd9 is played with your little finger off the guitar.

LEARN G CHORD
THE RIGHT WAY

G
CHORD
FULLY EXPLAINED

G	G	G
YES	YES	NO

There are two ways to play G chord. I am going to show them to you exactly as played by professional guitarists. Even if you have just started it is my experience that the best approach is to learn both positions from the start. Why? Because
1, it makes it much easier to speed up your changes in the early weeks of learning,
2, it also makes it a lot easier to add ornamentation and bass runs through your full chord sequences in a few months time, and
3, It opens up endless possibilities when you are a competent guitarist.

If you have been shown a G chord using the first, second, and third fingers, (a beginners G) I urge you to stop playing it this way from here on. It is not a good long term approach for four very good reasons.

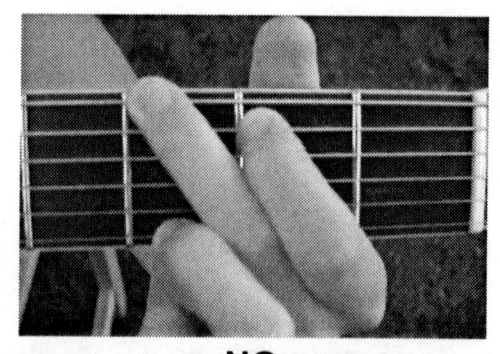

NO

IF YOU HAVE LEARNED, HAVE BEEN SHOWN, OR ARE PLAYING THIS G
PLEASE CHANGE IT NOW.

IT IS A SHORT TERM SOLUTION THAT BRINGS WITH IT LONG TERM PROBLEMS.

1. It cannot be developed further later. It just ends up being one sound.
2. It makes changing to D and C chords unnecessarily difficult and practically impossible for a beginner.
3. When you move to advanced guitar you will have to unlearn it in order to progress. So why learn it in the first place.
4. It is my personal experience that learning G this way is the third biggest reason why students get disillusioned with playing guitar.

If you have been playing for a while, and have been using this G, I urge you to stop now and relearn G as outlined in these pages. I can promise you five things if you learn G this way
You will find it much easier to quickly change to D, and C, in a few weeks time.
It will sound much better in a few weeks.
You will not have to relearn it later.
You will have the option later to include ornamentation, and bass runs.
It is exactly as used by professional players.

To differentiate between both G's we will call them G1 and G2, but both variations are really just called G. Later on you will know when and where to use each one.

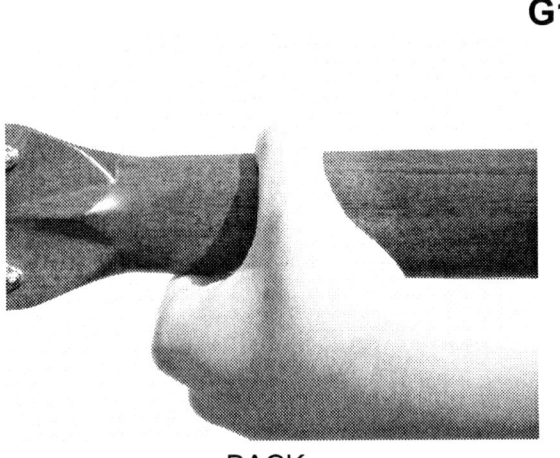

G1

BACK   FRONT

- **Position your thumb on top over the second fret.**
  It is touching the sixth string.

- **Place your first finger on the fifth string second fret**

- **Add your second finger on the sixth string, third fret.**

- **Add your third finger on the second string, third fret.**

- Add your fourth (little) finger on the first string third fret.
- Look at your fingers and say to yourself, or in your mind, G 1
- Take your fingers off the guitar.
- Start again, first with your thumb, then the fingers, and then say G 1 to help memorize the chord.

Keep repeating this sequence until you can find the chord without having to look at the picture.

G2

BACK   FRONT

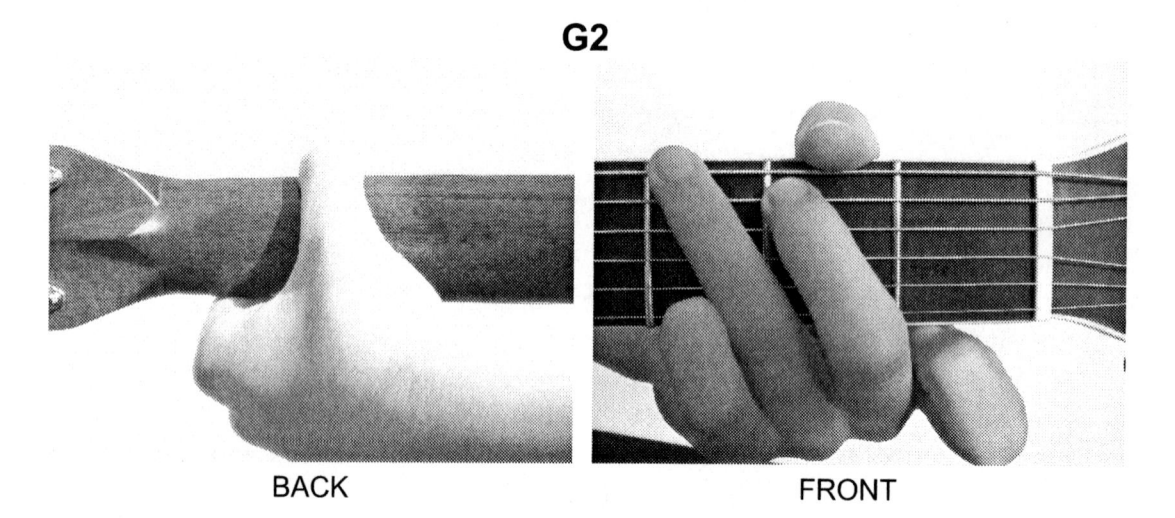

- **Position your thumb on top over the second fret.**
  It is touching the sixth string.
- **Place your second finger on the fifth string second fret**
- **Add your third finger on the sixth string, third fret.**
- **Add your fourth (little) finger on the first string third fret.**
- **Look at your fingers and say to yourself, or in your mind,** G 2
- **Take your fingers off the guitar.**
- **Start again, first with your thumb, then the fingers, and then say** G 2 **to help memorize the chord.**

Keep repeating this sequence until you can find the chord without having to look at the picture.

FOCUS POINT FOR STUDENTS AND TEACHERS

If you have a small hand and cannot get your thumb fully on top of your guitar just place it as near as possible to these positions. In a few months time you will find it a bit easier to do this.

If you are somebody who is trying to change from faulty thumb positioning to this you may experience poorer quality sound for a week or two. There is nothing to worry about when this happens. It is a sign of real progress and when your sound returns it will be much better and brighter than before.

Learning G the right way from the start will;
1. Open many doors to great guitar playing, and
2. Make the hardest change of all for beginners to master (G to D) much easier to overcome.

VERY IMPORTANT
PLAYING TECHNIQUE
The fifth string never sounds when you strum a G chord.

It only rings in a song when you are playing a bass run. When you fret a G you should notice that the inside of the finger on the top string is touching the fifth string, and automatically muting it. From this position you will be able to strum all six strings and yet only hear sound on the five you need, ie, 6th, 4th, 3rd, 2nd, and 1st. This is exactly how professional guitarists play G. You will never hear the fifth string ring and yet they are strumming all six strings. Take up your guitar for a minute and try it. Not alone does it sound a lot better, and clearer, it is actually much easier to do. Now forget the old way. This is how you will sound a G chord for the rest of your life.

This is yet again one of the invisible skills of great guitar playing. It cannot be picked up with the naked eye, and because the great players take it for granted, they forget to show it to you.

A QUESTION THAT I HAVE BEEN ASKED A THOUSAND TIMES

WHEN I PLAY G CHORD
WHY DO I HAVE TO MUTE THE SIXTH STRING, SECOND FRET, WITH MY THUMB WHEN THE SOUND IS COMING FROM THE SIXTH STRING THIRD FRET?

The reason why professional guitarists make it look so easy is that when changing chords they have eliminated all unnecessary movement. Everything is simplified down to a fine art, exactly as described all through this book. They know that the most consistent way to produce pure sound is to put the thumb on the sixth string on all chords except E type chords, eg E, Em, Em7 E9, etc.

Here is
a guiding principle
for life

If you want proof just turn on your tv and watch a professional.

ON ALL E TYPE CHORDS
THE THUMB DOES <u>NOT MUTE</u> THE SIXTH STRING.

ON ALL OTHER CHORDS
THE THUMB <u>MUTES</u> THE SIXTH STRING.

This is one of many reasons I have to get your thumb involved from the start. As I said earlier, without good thumb positioning we will never make it. With it anything is possible.

ANOTHER GREAT ADVANTAGE
OF LEARNING G
THE RIGHT WAY

The other amazing thing about this approach is that by keeping the thumb on G it is already in the correct position when you change to any other chord, except of course E's, where you simply lift the thumb slightly. You will not have to move your thumb each time you change thus eliminating a lot of unnecessary movement. Once you master this technique, It is actually a lot easier than what lesser guitarists do which is moving it off and on every time they change.

And what happens when they forget to move the thumb. It sounds awful. Even if a professional forgets it still sounds good. Because the thumb was already in position when he, or she changed chords, they actually had nothing to do in the first place. The next time you are at a concert or watching tv look out for this and you will see everything very differently.

YET ANOTHER GREAT ADVANTAGE
OF LEARNING G
THE RIGHT WAY

Have you noticed how good guitarists often are not looking at their guitar while they are playing? But if you look closer you will also notice how their thumb is staying very close to the position we have described here. From this starting point the fingers are doing all the work. Just like a ship the thumb is the anchor that keeps the fingers in position.

PLAYING YOUR GUITAR WITHOUT LOOKING AT IT

We all want to be able to play guitar without looking at it. It is one of every beginner's dreams. I know from years working with students of guitar that if you are a beginner, or improver that you will have tried to play without looking at your guitar, and missed the strings you meant to play.

Please go back and try this again after you have developed these skills. It will only take a few weeks. The next time you play your guitar without looking at it you will have much success, and the added bonus of closing your eyes to feel the music vibrate through you. This is yet another of the invisible skills of great playing.

**Your thumb is the great key
to being able to
play guitar without looking at it.
It is now your reference point.**

FOCUS POINT FOR STUDENTS AND TEACHERS

The way G chord is played, and how the thumb is used are two of the great differences between competent and incompetent guitarists.

If you have been playing what I call "the wrong G" in this book I urge you to stop now. It is a short term solution that will lead to long term problems. The professional approach I have outlined may be harder to learn, but only for one month. Once you have mastered these techniques the guitar will sound better, and be easier to play for the rest of your life.

MOON ROSE

GUITAR
PRACTICE PROGRAM
LESSON SEVEN

THE ROAD TO SUCCESS IS ALWAYS UNDER CONSTRUCTION

1. CHECK YOUR SET UP — GUITAR SLIGHTLY TILTED BACK TO YOU

2. POSTURE CHECK — SIT TALL, HEAD UP, STRAIGHT BACK

3. THUMB EXERCISE 1 — FIVE TIMES.

4. THUMB EXERCISE 2 — FIVE TIMES

5. TUCK GUITAR UNDER STRUMMING ARM.

6. FINGER EXERCISE 1 — AT LEAST TWICE EACH DAY. PRESS HARDER WITH YOUR FINGERS AND SPEED IT UP SLIGHTLY.

7. PRACTICE EM, D, AND D SUS4, C, C ADD9, AND BOTH G CHORDS — UNTIL YOU CAN DO THEM WITHOUT HAVING TO LOOK IN THE BOOK.

8. RHYTHM EXERCISE 1 — PRACTICE STRUMMING. MAKE SURE THE STRINGS ARE VAMPED WITH YOUR FRETTING HAND. STRUM FIRST OF ALL ON YOUR OWN, AND THEN TO YOUR FAVOURITE CD'S.

9. CHECK THUMB POSITION ON CHORDS.

10. PLAY CHORDS WITH YOUR FRETTING HAND, AND STRUM THE GUITAR. IS IT TUCKED UNDER YOUR ARM?

11. PLACE PLEC BACK BETWEEN THE STRINGS WHEN YOU FINISH.

12. FILL IN YOUR PROGRESS CHART.

MOON ROSE

GUITAR LESSON EIGHT

YOUR RHYTHM HAND.

ALL GUITAR RHYTHMS STARTS HERE.
THE WRONG WAY TO LEARN GUITAR RHYTHMS
THE RIGHT WAY TO LEARN GUITAR RHYTHMS
THE SECRET
ITS SO SIMPLE YOU WILL MISS IT. MOST DO
GUITAR RHYTHMS THAT YOU CAN USE IN THOUSANDS OF SONGS

RHYTHM GUITAR

If your timing is perfect you will be able to
play guitar with all competent musicians, and
rhythm sections, (ie; drums and bass) all over the world.
If your timing is the slightest bit out
you will end up playing on your own.

ALL GUITAR RHYTHMS START HERE

I showed you a very simple rhythm technique in lesson four. It is actually where all rhythm guitar songs begin. While it is a very powerful learning technique, it is too basic to perform live. Your audience will either fall asleep, or go elsewhere, and we don't want that to happen. However if you have not been practicing this exercise please go back now. It is a very simple, realistic, and achievable step for all guitarists. But without it you will not be able to time the next four rhythms properly.

When we start learning guitar most of us tend to work on our fretting hand a lot, and not so much on rhythms. This is a very natural tendency as rhythms seem to be a matter of just strumming up and down, and up and down. There has never been, or never will be a good rhythm guitarist who can play without listening at the same time. Therefore we have to learn to play with our hands and our ears at the same time.

Also many of us want to play now. So we try instantly to play with both hands at the same time and what happens? Because we are trying to do too much, our self esteem takes a pounding and many of us give up at this point. This is another reason why so many of us hit a wall when we try to play more advanced arrangements of songs, and find it so difficult to play along with cd's, or other musicians.

If we stay focused on your rhythm hand only for a few minutes to point you in the right direction it will prove very beneficial no matter how much progress you make on your instrument. The four exercises I am going to show you are a foundation to every song that ever was, or will be strummed on guitar. They are often used by working guitarists when they have to play a song but do not know the actual recorded rhythm. No matter what song you try to learn it can be traced back to one or more of these rhythms in some shape or form.

Therefore it is a logical step to get you started from here too. Once you get good at playing them on your own you could then practice to your favorite cd's. As we said earlier this makes you play with your hands, and your ears.

THE WRONG WAY TO LEARN GUITAR RHYTHMS

The easy way of learning rhythms is to have arrows on a page and strum down, up, down etc. This might be good for your self esteem after you have just started. In the long term this approach is very, very destructive. How do I know this?

It is my experience that all guitarists who start this way hit a wall a few months later and cannot crack the more syncopated professional rhythms. I have had hundreds of students like this coming to me over the years. They were stuck, and could not progress any further from where they were. The only way we could achieve success is when we deprogrammed their faults, then went right back to the beginning, and learned properly.

If you have been playing guitar before you got this book and feel that this might be you I urge you for the next few weeks to slowly practice the following exercises slowly, and perfectly. It will seem very difficult at first but I promise you they work. Remember, if we don't change we will get what we already have. People have come to me about their timing saying that they are hopeless cases. They were up to then a helpless case, but a hopeless case, never.

> There is no such thing as a hopeless case;
> especially when it comes to learning guitar.

THE RIGHT WAY TO LEARN GUITAR RHYTHMS

THE SECRET
IT IS SO SIMPLE YOU WILL MISS IT.
MOST DO.

All guitar rhythms come from one, and only one foundation rhythm pattern. Most of you will find this almost impossible to believe. But it's true. It is an optical illusion. Even though songs sound different all great guitarists use the same approach either consciously, or subconsciously, song after song, night after night, year after year.

The best way to get good at something is to keep doing the same thing over, and over, and over. If you are doing a different thing every five minutes, or every night you are never going to get very good at anything. So if we can have the same approach to all our rhythms we have a much better chance of becoming good rhythm guitarists. How is this done? Here is a step by step guide.

STARTING POSITION  | DOWNSTROKE HAND GOING DOWN | UPSTROKE HAND GOING UP

MOON ROSE GUITAR
RHYTHM EXERCISE I
AND THE SECRET
THE FOUNDATION RHYTHM FOR ALL SONGS

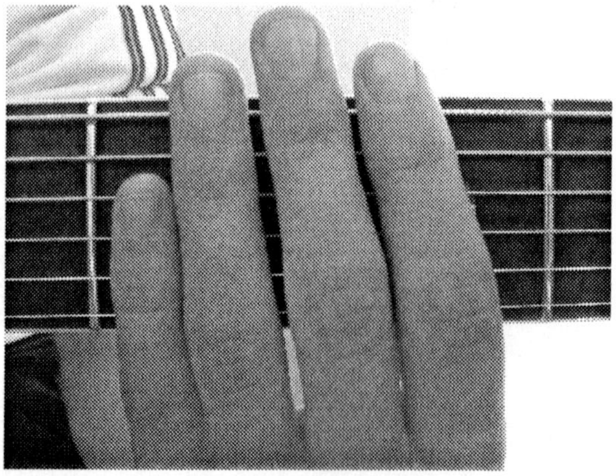

1. Mute the strings as in rhythm exercise 1 Your fingers should be barely touching the strings to eliminate sound. Now you will be able to perfect rhythms quicker because you do not have the added pressure of playing the chords. You will also be instantly able to play along with cd's.

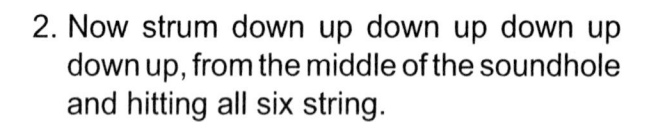

2. Now strum down up down up down up down up, from the middle of the soundhole and hitting all six string.

3. Instead of counting 1, 2, 3, 4, can you very slowly count 1 and 2 and 3 and 4 and 1 and 2 and 3 and 4 and (keep repeating)

4. Then tap your foot as you keep counting 1 and 2 and 3 and 4 and.

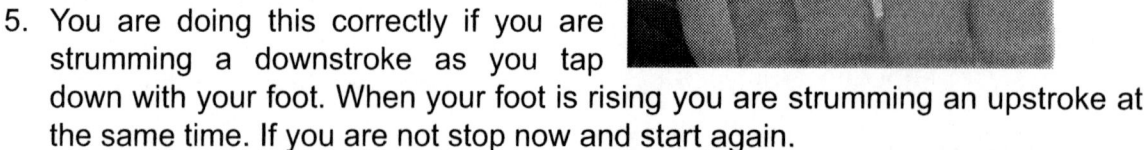

5. You are doing this correctly if you are strumming a downstroke as you tap down with your foot. When your foot is rising you are strumming an upstroke at the same time. If you are not stop now and start again.

6. The slower you do this exercise in the beginning the quicker you will master it. If you cannot do it slow, it is a guarantee that you cannot do it fast.

7. Now keep strumming, and foot tapping, and counting, but instead of hitting the strings just miss them as you go up and down.

8. Then can you keep repeating this without stopping;

                   go 1 and 2 and 3 and 4 and (hitting the stings)
   and then   go 1 and 2 and 3 and 4 and (missing the stings)
   and then   go 1 and 2 and 3 and 4 and (hitting the stings)
   and then   go 1 and 2 and 3 and 4 and (missing the stings)

9. Finally, instead of using a plectrum you can use your thumb for downstrokes and your first finger for upstrokes. If you go back and repeat this exercise with your thumb and first finger instead of a plectrum you will have yet another skill needed for good guitar playing. When you become a competent guitarist you will have the option to play songs with a plectrum or with your fingers. It will also help greatly when you start to play more advanced fingerstyle guitar.

PERFECTING
THE OPTICAL ILLUSION

Can you, if possible, look at yourself in a large mirror doing this exercise? From a distance your eyes will not notice the big difference between the two strum patterns. To approach all guitar rhythms correctly;

1. Always use this strum pattern
2. Hit the strings when an arrow is indicated
3. Miss the strings when no arrow is indicated.

This is what all good guitarists do, either consciously, or unconsciously. Once you familiarize yourself with this vital skill you will never go back. You will suddenly see that you now have one approach, and one pattern for all rhythms.

You will also see that you only have to speed it up for fast songs, and slow it down for slow songs. The length of the stroke will vary (it wont always be six strings) but this exercise takes care of that too.

FOCUS POINT FOR STUDENTS AND TEACHERS

This is one of the great invisible skills of real quality guitar playing. It is so simple most people miss it. I have witnessed this exercise help put students on the right road from the beginning. More importantly, when it came to learning more complicated rhythms later on, they were now equipped to master them.

If you are playing guitar for a while and have not used this approach to learning rhythms I urge you to do so as soon as possible. While it is more difficult in the beginning and harder to master in the first two weeks, it is far more beneficial in the long term. As it is a foundation to all rhythms it opens up endless possibilities for a lifetime.

GUITAR RHYTHMS
YOU CAN USE IN THOUSANDS OF SONGS

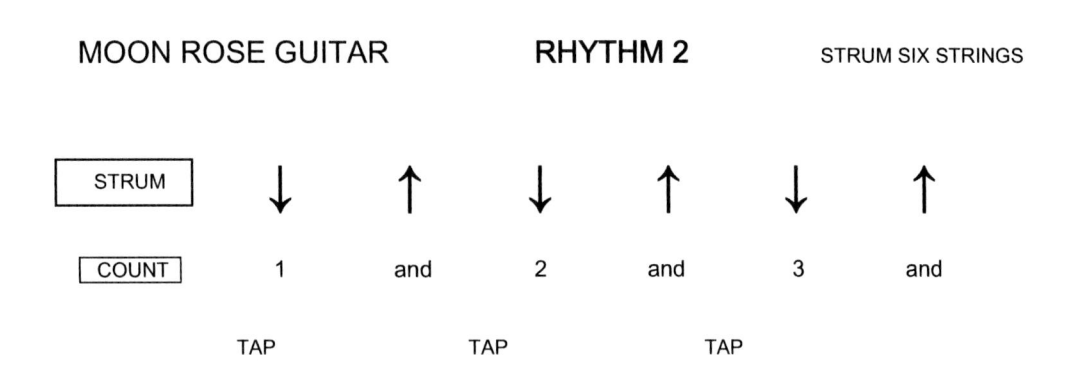

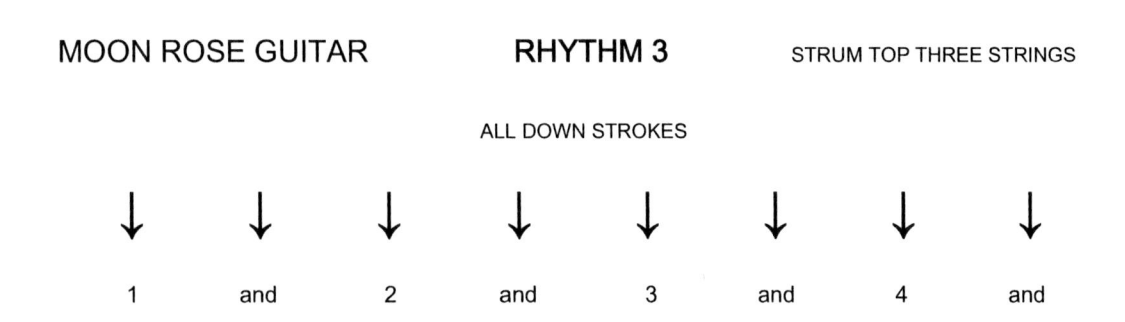

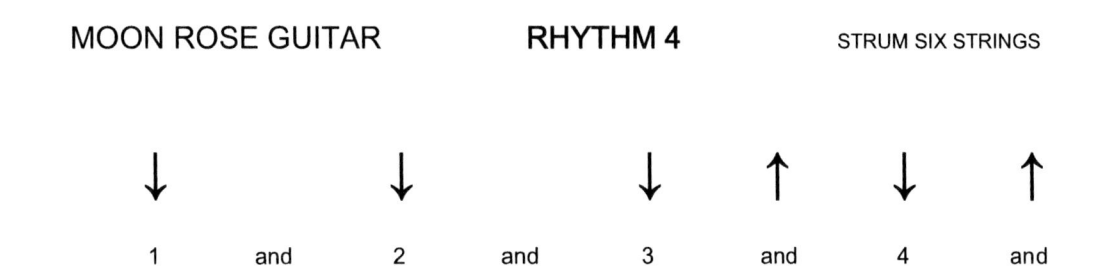

MOON ROSE GUITAR   **RHYTHM 2**   STRUM SIX STRINGS

STRUM	↓	↑	↓	↑	↓	↑
COUNT	1	and	2	and	3	and

TAP   TAP   TAP

MOON ROSE GUITAR   **RHYTHM 3**   STRUM TOP THREE STRINGS

ALL DOWN STROKES

↓   ↓   ↓   ↓   ↓   ↓   ↓   ↓

1 and 2 and 3 and 4 and

MOON ROSE GUITAR   **RHYTHM 4**   STRUM SIX STRINGS

↓   ↓   ↓   ↑   ↓   ↑

1 and 2 and 3 and 4 and

MOON ROSE

GUITAR
PRACTICE PROGRAM
MOON ROSE
LESSON EIGHT

TEMPORARY DEFEAT IS NOT PERMANENT FAILURE

1. CHECK YOUR SET UP — GUITAR SLIGHTLY TILTED BACK TO YOU

2. POSTURE CHECK — SIT TALL, HEAD UP, STRAIGHT BACK

3. THUMB EXERCISE 1 — FIVE TIMES.

4. THUMB EXERCISE 2 — FIVE TIMES

5. TUCK GUITAR UNDER STRUMMING ARM.

6. FINGER EXERCISE 1 — AT LEAST TWICE EACH DAY. KEEP PRESSING HARD AND TRY TO MOVE YOUR FINGERS TO THE CORNER OF EACH FRET.

7. PRACTICE EM, D, AND D SUS4, C, C ADD9, AND BOTH G CHORDS — UNTIL YOU CAN DO THEM WITHOUT HAVING TO LOOK IN THE BOOK.

8. RHYTHM EXERCISES — PRACTICE STRUMMING USING A PLECTRUM. MAKE SURE THE STRINGS ARE VAMPED WITH YOUR FRETTING HAND. STRUM FIRST OF ALL ON YOUR OWN, AND THEN TO YOUR FAVOURITE CD'S.

9. NOW REPEAT THIS EXERCISE WITHOUT THE PLECTRUM. USE YOUR THUMB FOR DOWNSTROKES AND YOUR FIRST FINGER FOR UPSTROKES.

10. CHECK THUMB POSITION ON CHORDS.

11. PLAY CHORDS WITH YOUR FRETTING HAND, AND STRUM THE GUITAR. IS IT TUCKED UNDER YOUR ARM? YOUR GUITAR SHOULD BE SOUNDING A LITTLE BETTER NOW.

12. PLACE PLEC BACK BETWEEN THE STRINGS WHEN YOU FINISH.

13. FILL IN YOUR PROGRESS CHART.

MOON ROSE

GUITAR LESSON NINE

IMPROVING YOUR SOUND

ANOTHER SECRET
THE AMATEUR APPROACH TO GOOD SOUND
THE PROFESSIONAL APPROACH TO GOOD SOUND

IMPROVING YOUR SOUND

Developing pure sound is one of the two big hurdles we face when learning guitar. We can be very close to playing good guitar but it will not sound good until we learn how to produce a nice clear sound. A lot of us assume that if we press harder with our fingers we should have a better sound. Unfortunately this is not the case for two reasons.

1. When we press harder with your fretting hand almost all of us strum harder with our other hand, and it becomes very noisy and loud. If you listen to a recording you will notice that even if the guitar is loud it is not strummed loud most of the time. Whether it is electric or acoustic it is strummed nice and soft. With our finger exercise we are making our fingers independent of each other.

ANOTHER SECRET

Now, in order to sound good we have to make our two hands independent of each other. Your fretting hand will have to press hard on the strings while the other hands strum softly. This is yet another of the great invisible skills of professional guitar playing. It is in all songs right from the start. The lighter you can strum while you are perfecting this skill, the quicker your progress will be.

2. Your thumb action is critical to producing good sound. This is one of the reasons why I put the thumb exercise at the very start. From here on, if your hand is big enough, your thumb should mute, or touch the sixth string for all chords, except E type chords. If you do not believe me the next time you are watching a good guitarist, either at a show, or on TV, watch the thumb. At the moment when the sixth string sounds it compliments E type chords only. It sounds dreadful with all the other chords as it is not musically correct.

THE AMATEUR APPROACH

The amateur approach here is to strum four or maybe five strings for D, or C, or any chord, except E, Em, or E7 where you strum six strings. Because we are human and will always make the odd mistake this skill is impossible to perfect in the long term.

THE PROFESSIONAL APPROACH

The professional knows that if the sixth string is continuously muted by the thumb it will never sound whether it is strummed, or not. The thumb is like an insurance policy that protects you from the horrible booming sound. Now, all they do is release the thumb for E type chords and they will get the desired six string sound, and the thumb drops back onto the top string once they are gone to another chord.

They also now have the huge advantage of being able to strum six strings for all chords, unlike the amateur approach. The professional approach is actually much easier if you take the time to perfect it. Now your strumming hand is doing the same thing for all chords.

Everything I am showing you in this book is exactly as played by professional guitarists. If you are a beginner do not worry. As I said before I am keeping you very much in mind all through writing this book. Developing good sound will be easier than you think. If you have been following our practice programme I laid it out in such a way as to make this stage as easy as possible. I could not tell you this at the start but I do have a vast amount of experience working with people like yourself. Hopefully you will trust me. There is no short cut around this hurdle but my experience is helping you to multi task as much as possible, so please hang in there. If you are still following the practice programme there is a lot more happening than you now realize. It is only when you look back in six months time, and reread some of this book that you will fully appreciate it. I have never wasted as much as one minute of anyone's time practicing something unnecessary. I will not waste your time either. The next exercise is going to give you three vital ingredients that are in all songs.

It will

1. Give you the correct strength in the fingers of your fretting hand.

2. Make both hands independent of each other.

3. You will press hard on the strings, but strum softly, when you play songs, one of the invisible skills of all great guitar playing.

MOON ROSE GUITAR
FINGER EXERCISE 2
THESE SKILLS WILL LAST A LIFETIME

THEY ARE IN EVERY SONG
THAT EVER WAS OR WILL BE
PLAYED ON GUITAR

This is similar to exercise one but there are a few differences and it will be more difficult to do for a few days. Instead of starting at the top we are now starting at the bottom, and also picking the strings, as in the photo sequence. When picking individual strings on the guitar your hand should rest on the bridge as in the pictures. This skill is explained in more detail later on in this lesson. It is a vital fundamental of lead guitar and fingerstyle guitar playing. You may not fully appreciate it today as you are not used to it. But I promise you that keeping your hand on the bridge through this exercise opens many doors to great guitar playing.

When you bring the first finger up to the second string can you pick it with your plectrum? You may have to pick it a few times pressing harder each time to get a good quality sound. Can you also make sure that your finger is in the corner of the fret? Now you should not have to press so hard. Then bring the second finger up to the second string and pick it. Once you have a sound you can bring the third finger up, then the fourth.

Now go back to the first finger and move it up to the third string. Keep going until you reach the top string as in the finger sequence, or until you get cramp in the back of your hand. If this happens, stop and rest for a few minutes. You will get further each time you do it, and in a few weeks it will be effortless.

Now stop reading and try to practice this exercise a few times.

STARTING POSITION

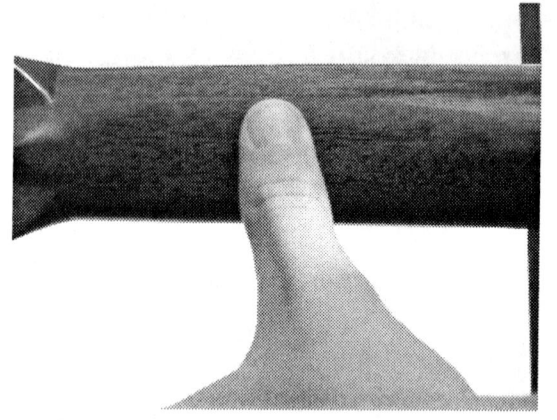

THUMB LOW AND CENTERED

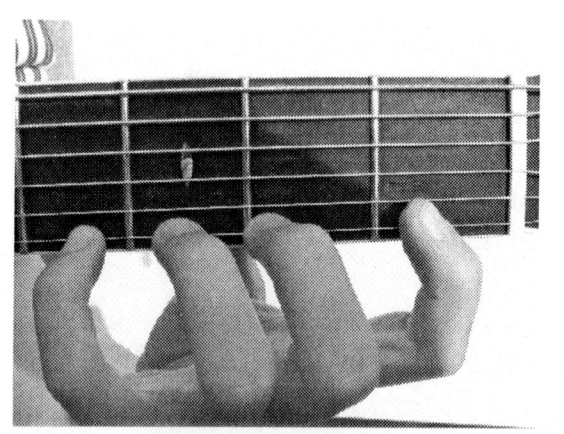

FOUR FINGERS
ON FIRST STRING

PICKING HAND
ON BRIDGE

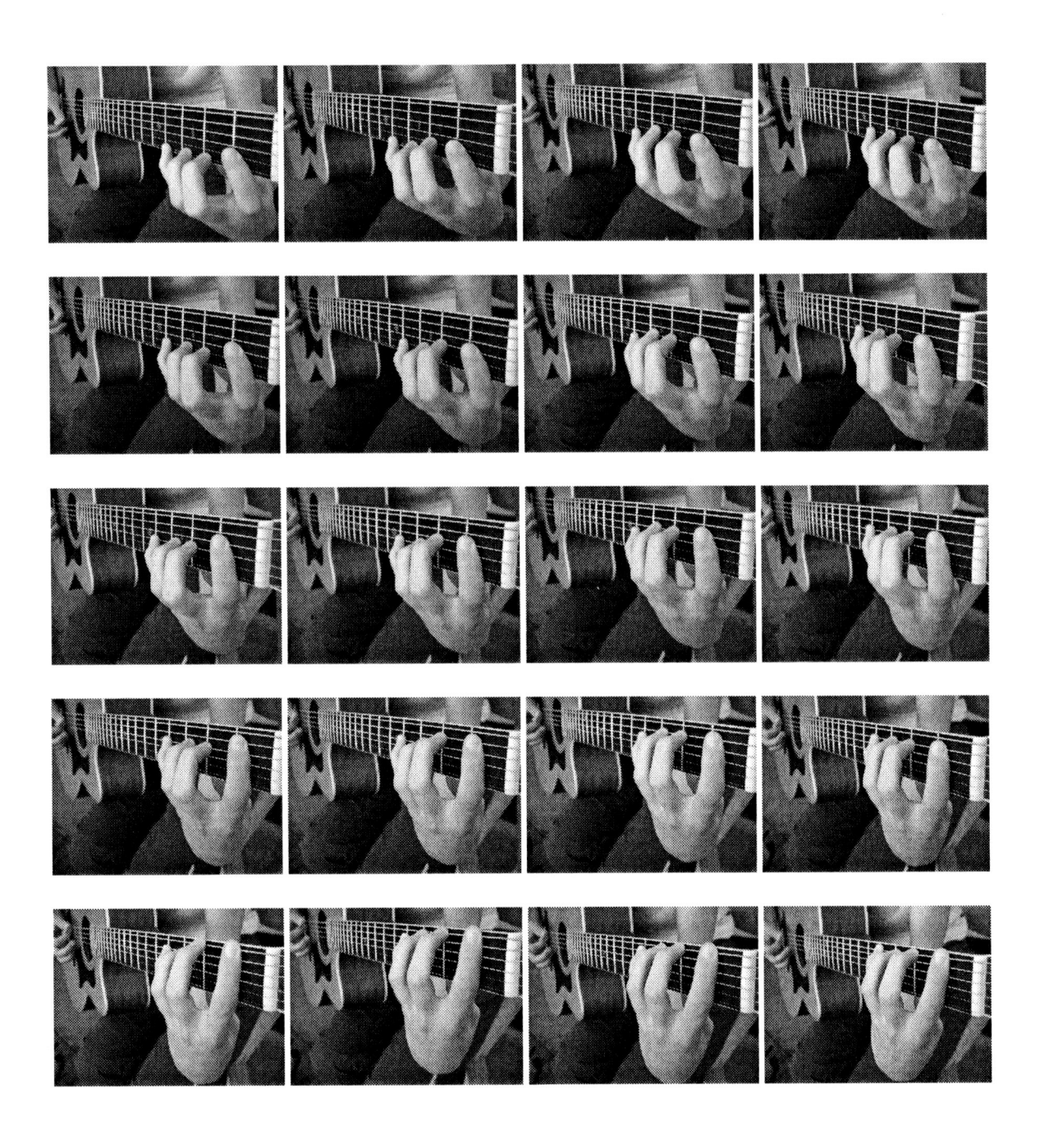

Tough going, isn't it". Did you notice how much harder you had to press to produce a clear sound? That is the amount of pressure you need when playing chords. From now on when you practice a song can you make sure that you are pressing harder with your chords, and also strumming softer? I understand that you might think it is too hard to do but after a few weeks you will be pressing hard but it will feel natural. Most importantly your guitar will sound big, bright, and better than ever before.

The good news is that once you have mastered this you have it for life. You will not need to practice it any more. Just keep playing your favorite songs.

ALL LEAD GUITAR AND FINGERSTYLE GUITAR ALSO STARTS HERE.

IT IS YOUR REFERENCE POINT.

YES   **YES**

Lead guitar   **Finger style guitar**

Lead guitar and finger style guitar hand position the very same.

NO

Many people start off by picking either with a plectrum or their fingers from this position. Again it is a short term solution that brings with it long term problems. Even though the way I am showing you here is harder to learn for about a week it is much easier once you have got used to it. If you don't believe me ask any professional guitarist or turn on your tv tonight and try to observe these skills.

FOCUS POINT FOR STUDENTS AND TEACHERS

The ability to pick individual strings while keeping your hand on the bridge is a priceless skill. It is not as simple as it looks. When you try this exercise you will notice a pull on your picking hand. For a few nights you will notice how it has moved up towards the soundhole without you noticing it. When this happens STOP. Now go back and start again. Soon you will notice that it has finally stayed on the bridge all through the exercise. The ability to play lead and fingerstyle guitar from the bridge position is a priceless skill and will make your musical journey much more enjoyable. Once you have it you will not want to go back and it will last a lifetime.

Now you have developed another invaluable skill that all professionals use.
For all lead lines, hooks, and fills, in almost all songs the rhythm hand plays from the bridge.
For almost all songs where you are strumming the rhythm hand plays from near the soundhole.

Being able to play lead lines and hooks from the bridge allows you to play with speed and accuracy. When you are competent you will have the huge advantage of not having to look at your picking hand any longer. Because you are playing from just one position it is almost impossible to make a mistake.

The next time you watch a good guitarist you will notice that they only look at the fretting hand if they have to move it up or down the neck when playing a lead line. They will never look at the picking hand because it is on the bridge.

FOCUS POINT FOR STUDENTS AND TEACHERS

Because we are now moving up a level it is very important that we perfect this exercise slowly for a few days with much attention to detail. The most important points to remember as you practice are;

- PICKING HAND ON BRIDGE
- THUMB WELL POSITIONED BEHIND NECK
- FINGERS IN CORNER OF FRETS
- PRESS EACH NOTE HARD
- PICK SOFTLY
- MOVING ONLY ONE FINGER AT A TIME

You will feel your fingertips getting sore again. They are now hardening to the levels needed to produce clear sound. It could be a little painful for a week but it is well worth it when you make it. If you have been playing already but struggled to get speed and accuracy on lead lines, it is more than likely that your hand was not on the bridge of the guitar. If this is so, could you go back and try them again once you have familiarized yourself with this new position. I believe it will, in time, give you speed, accuracy, and the ability to play without looking at the strings.

A SIMPLE BUT INVALUABLE RHYTHM HAND EXERCISE

Professional guitarists use two rhythm hand positions for almost all songs. Here they are.

Lead guitar and Finger style guitar

Rhythm guitar

Now here is a simple exercise that will help you perfect them as quick as possible.

MOON ROSE
GUITAR RHYTHM
EXERCISE FIVE

- Vamp the strings with your fretting hand.
- Place your rhythm hand on the bridge and pick any one string up and down as fast as you can.
- Now strum your guitar from over the soundhole up and down as fast as you can.
- Now place your rhythm hand back on the bridge and pick any one string up and down as fast as you can.
- Now strum your guitar again from over the soundhole up and down as fast as you can.
- Keep switching from one position to the other, while strumming and picking.

Now it is easy to perfect this very important skill because you do not have the added pressure of playing a song. When you advance, or observe a professional guitarist you will see that both positions are needed for good guitar playing.

MOON ROSE

GUITAR
PRACTICE PROGRAM
LESSON NINE

BELIEVE AND SUCCEED

1. CHECK YOUR SET UP — GUITAR SLIGHTLY TILTED BACK TO YOU

2. POSTURE CHECK — SIT TALL, HEAD UP, STRAIGHT BACK

3. THUMB EXERCISE 1 — FIVE TIMES.

4. THUMB EXERCISE 2 — FIVE TIMES

5. TUCK GUITAR UNDER STRUMMING ARM.

6. NEW FINGER EXERCISE 2 — AT LEAST TWICE EACH DAY. PICKING HAND MUST BE ON THE BRIDGE OF YOUR GUITAR. PICK STRINGS WITH YOUR PLECTRUM FROM HERE ON. KEEP PRESSING HARD AND TRY TO MOVE YOUR FINGERS TO THE CORNER OF EACH FRET.

7. RHYTHM EXERCISES — PRACTICE STRUMMING USING A PLECTRUM. MAKE SURE THE STRINGS ARE VAMPED WITH YOUR FRETTING HAND. STRUM FIRST OF ALL ON YOUR OWN, AND THEN TO YOUR FAVOURITE CD'S.

8. NOW REPEAT THIS EXERCISE WITHOUT THE PLECTRUM. USE YOUR THUMB FOR DOWNSTROKES AND YOUR FIRST FINGER FOR UPSTROKES.

9. NEW RHYTHM EXERCISE FIVE

10. CHECK THUMB POSITION ON CHORDS.

11. PLAY CHORDS WITH YOUR FRETTING HAND, AND STRUM THE GUITAR. IS IT TUCKED UNDER YOUR ARM? YOUR GUITAR SHOULD BE SOUNDING A LITTLE BETTER NOW.

12. PLACE PLEC BACK BETWEEN THE STRINGS WHEN YOU FINISH.

13. FILL IN YOUR PROGRESS CHART.

MOON ROSE

GUITAR LESSON TEN

FAST CHORD CHANGING

A SIMPLE YET POWERFUL
LEARNING AND TEACHING TECHNIQUE
SPEED UP THESE CHORD CHANGES IN ONE MINUTE
THE EASIEST CHANGES TO PERFECT ON GUITAR
F CHORD IS EASY BUT WHY IS IT SO HARD
A PRICELESS
LEARNING AND TEACHING TECHNIQUE
FOR BEGINNERS

A SIMPLE YET POWERFUL
LEARNING AND TEACHING TECHNIQUE

Can you copy this picture of Am7?

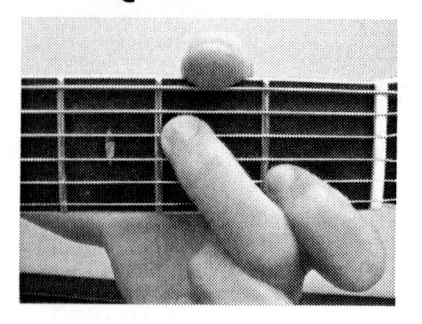

Then in your mind or out loud can you say Am7?

Now can you add your third finger on the fifth string third fret?

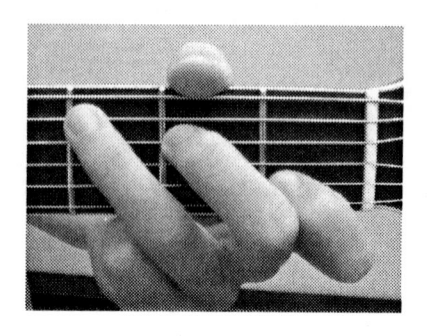

Then in your mind or out loud can you say C?

Now can you take your third finger off and you say Am7? Add it and say C.

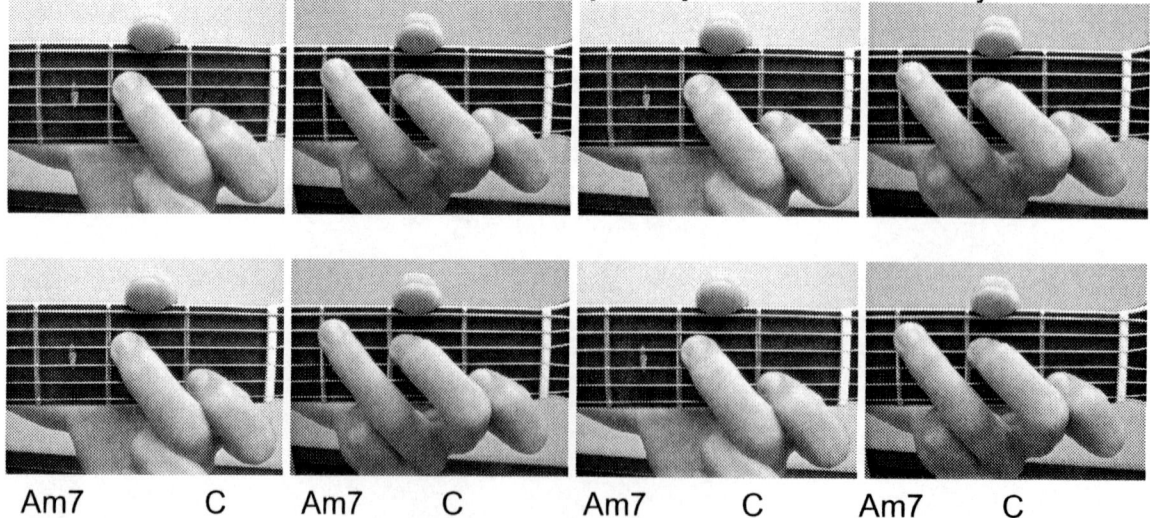

Am7   C   Am7   C   Am7   C   Am7   C

Why is this so good?
- You are now learning two chords off by heart.
- You have also perfected the chord change that is needed to play them in a song.
- That's as fast as it gets.

Why was this so easy to do? Because we have two pivot fingers. They were in the same position for both chords so there was no need to take them off the guitar to build the next chord. All professionals are masters at pivot fingering. It is a key reason why they can make something that sounds difficult look so easy. That is because it is easy.

Now I am going to show you the main chord changes where pivot fingering occurs. You will enjoy this because you will perfect each chord change less than sixty seconds.

SPEED UP THESE CHORD CHANGES IN ONE MINUTE

Can you make sure to say the names of each chord either in your mind or out loud as you practice? As well speeding up the change you are learning the chords off by heart just like a good guitarist.

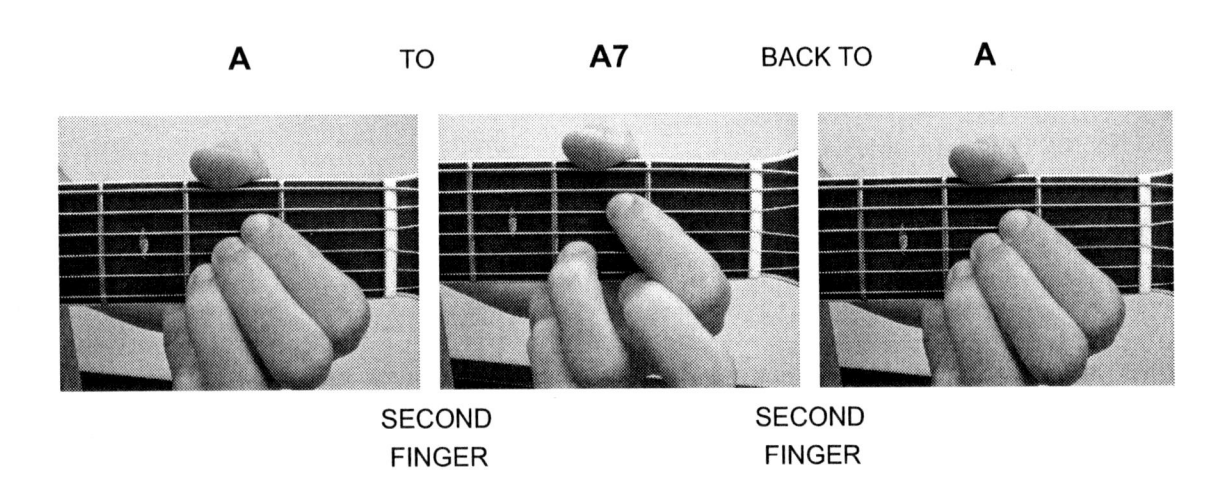

A TO **A7** BACK TO **A**

SECOND FINGER   SECOND FINGER

That was easy wasn't it? That is as fast as you need it. Lets try some more.

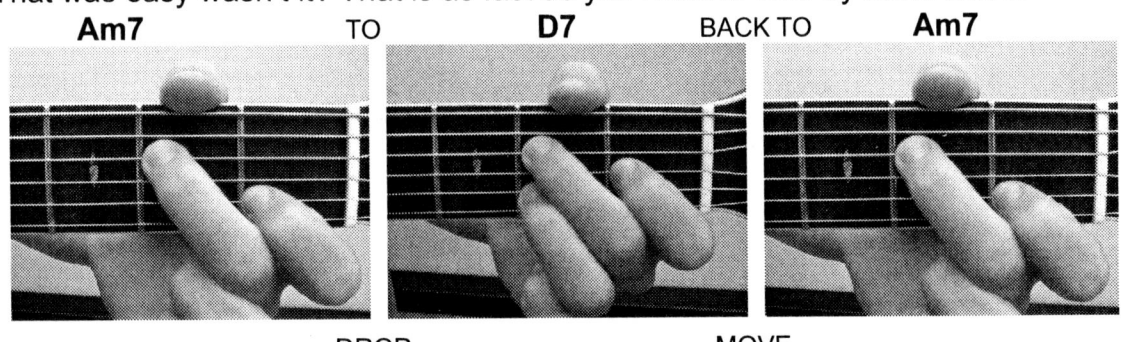

Am7 TO **D7** BACK TO **Am7**

DROP SECOND FINGER DOWN ONE STRING ADD THIRD FINGER ON FIRST STRING

MOVE SECOND FINGER UP ONE STRING AND TAKE OFF THIRD FINGER

Em   TO   **E9**   BACK TO   **Em**

DROP THIRD FINGER DOWN ONE STRING

MOVE THIRD FINGER UP ONE STRING

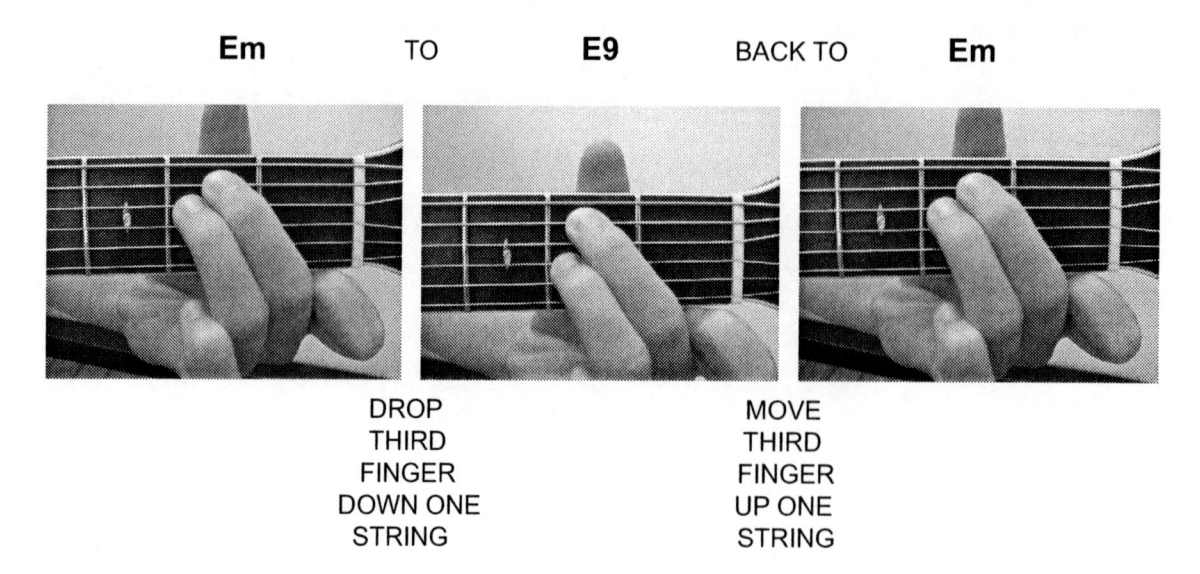

We are going great. Isn't it much easier to learn guitar when we work on each hand separately. Our progress is much faster too.

Let's try another one. This is slightly harder as we have only one pivot finger and we have to move two fingers.

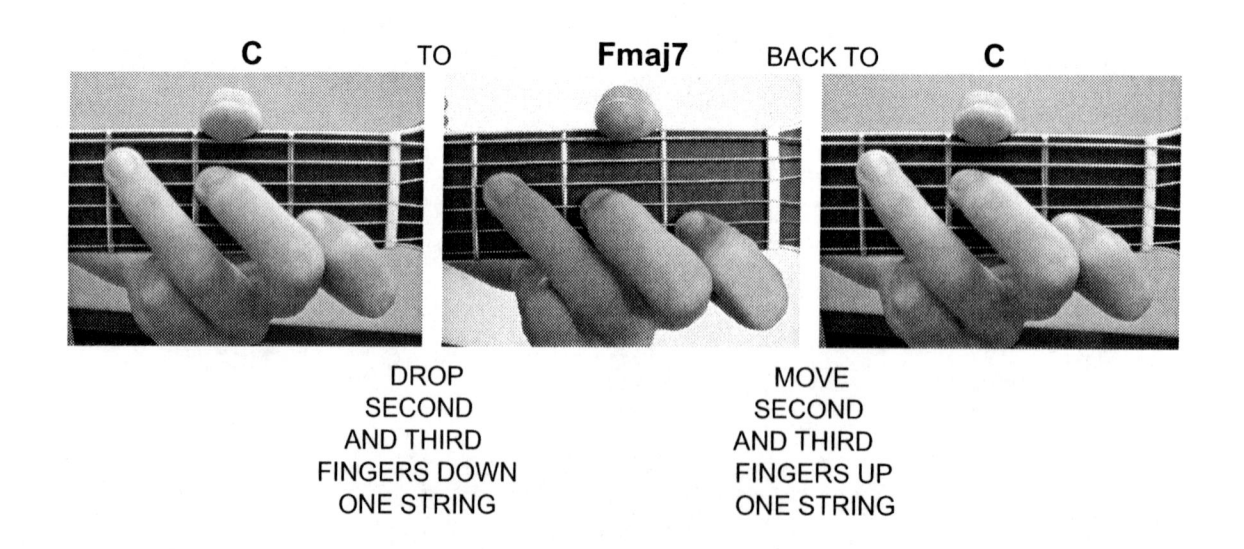

C   TO   **Fmaj7**   BACK TO   **C**

DROP SECOND AND THIRD FINGERS DOWN ONE STRING

MOVE SECOND AND THIRD FINGERS UP ONE STRING

D7   TO   **Fmaj7**   BACK TO   **D7**

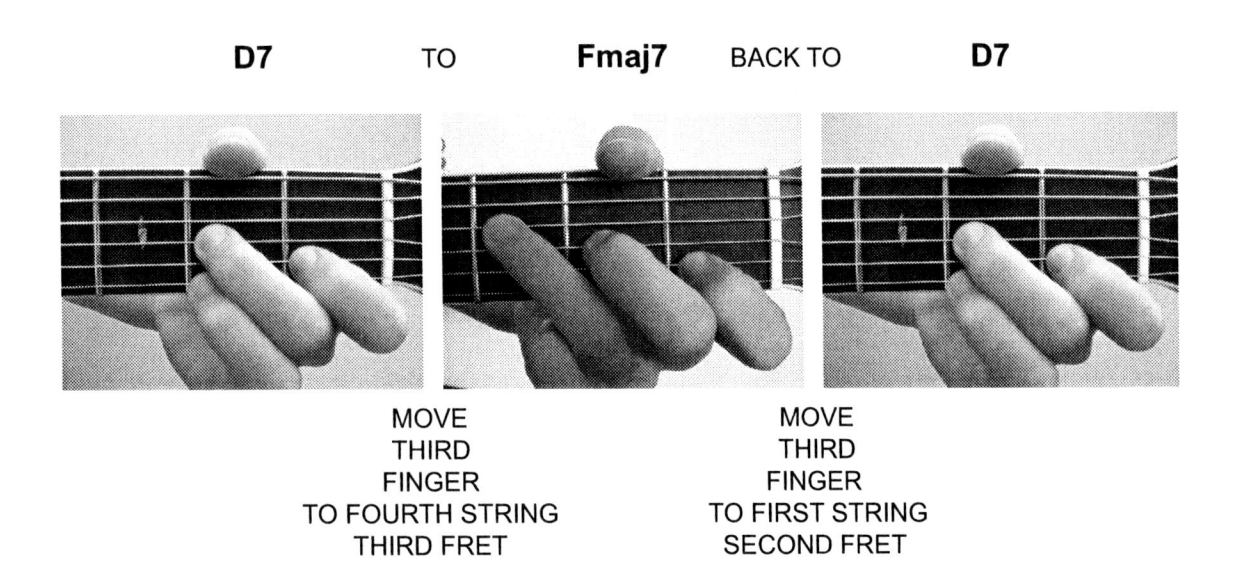

MOVE THIRD FINGER TO FOURTH STRING THIRD FRET

MOVE THIRD FINGER TO FIRST STRING SECOND FRET

F CHORD IS EASY BUT WHY IS IT SO HARD

If you have been playing for a while you might have tried an F chord. This is because so many real quality songs have an F we come across it sooner or later. Many of us find it very difficult. I will try to let you see what is really happening here.

Learning an F chord is easy. Even if you have never played before all you have to do is copy the picture in the back of this book. The difficulty is trying to change quickly into it during a song. My advice is perfect G, D, C, and Em first. Instead of F use an Fmajor7 and mute the first and sixth string until your fingers are stronger. It may not be exactly what is recorded in the song you are trying to learn but it is musically correct. More importantly it is realistic and attainable.

YOU CAN PLAY THOUSANDS OF SONGS WITHOUT MOVING YOUR THIRD FINGER

Can you take a look at these guitar chords? They all have four things in common.

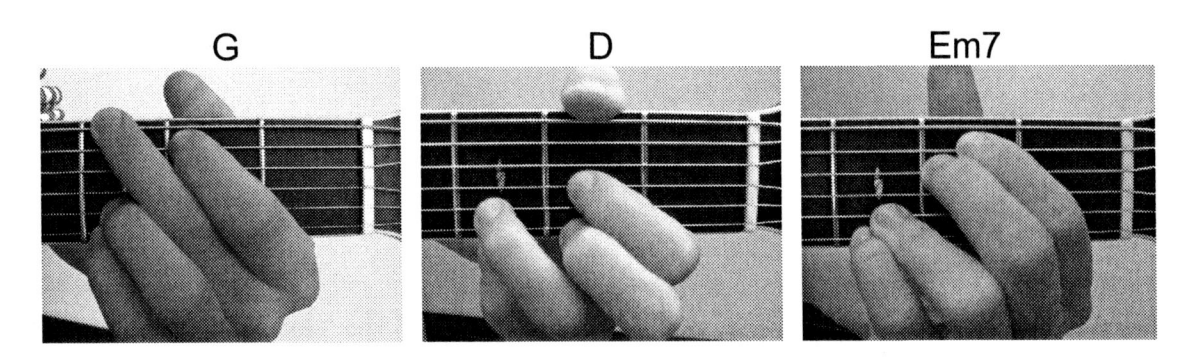

G   D   Em7

D/B   Cadd9   A7sus4

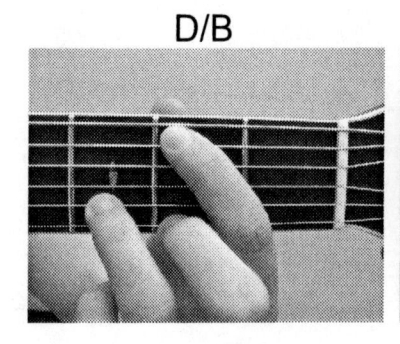

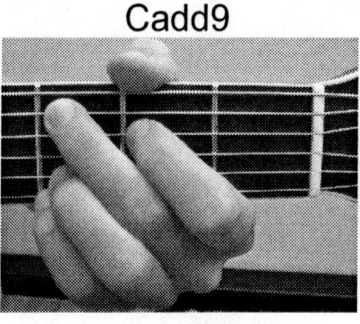

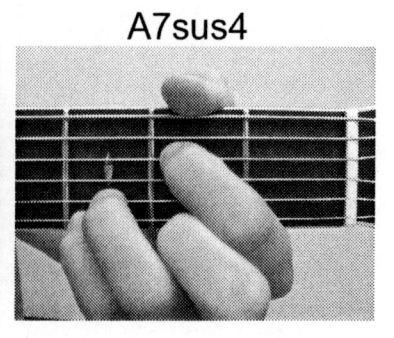

1. THESE CHORDS ARE IN THOUSANDS OF SONGS.

2. THE THIRD FINGER IS IN THE SAME POSITION FOR EACH CHORD.

3. THE THUMB HAS HARDLY MOVED. IT IS IN MUCH THE SAME POSITION IN EACH PICTURE.

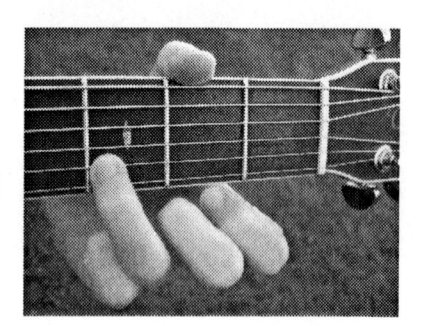

4. BECAUSE WE WILL NOT BE MOVING OUR THUMB OR OUR THIRD FINGER THESE SONGS ARE GOING TO BE MUCH EASIER TO PLAY.

Some of these chords have big fancy names. Many beginners' first impressions are that chords with fancy names must be harder to play. These are some of the easiest of all guitar chords once you know what you are doing. They are in thousands of songs, including many of the most famous songs of all time. Sweet Home Alabama, Wonderwall, and Free Falling, are just three that come to mind.

They are in many of the classics. If this is true, and it is, and if we know these chords and can change from one to the next quickly then haven't we a great chance of being able to play many of these of songs too? Yes we have.

The most productive way to practice these is as follows. Rather than pick one song with some of these chord changes our progress will be much faster by practicing them all together with our fretting hand only.

A PRICELESS
LEARNING AND TEACHING TECHNIQUE
FOR BEGINNERS

THE
MOON ROSE
GUITAR CHORD EXERCISE

Start with the first picture G.
Then slowly go to   D   without moving your thumb or third finger.
Then slowly go to   Em   without moving your thumb or third finger.
Then slowly go to   D/B   without moving your thumb or third finger.
Then slowly go to Cadd9 without moving your thumb or third finger.
Then slowly go to A7sus4 without moving your thumb or third finger.

I promise you that if you give a few minutes every day to this you will be absolutely amazed in a few weeks. The next time you are observing a professional guitarist you will clearly see this skill.

Once we are over this hurdle you are now ready to start downloading songs from the internet or using songbooks to start learning our own favorite songs.

MOON ROSE

GUITAR
PRACTICE PROGRAM
LESSON TEN

> EASY DOES IT

1. CHECK YOUR SET UP   GUITAR SLIGHTLY TILTED BACK TO YOU

2. POSTURE CHECK   SIT TALL, HEAD UP, STRAIGHT BACK

3. THUMB EXERCISE 1   FIVE TIMES.

4. THUMB EXERCISE 2   FIVE TIMES

5. TUCK GUITAR UNDER STRUMMING ARM.

6. NEW FINGER EXERCISE 2   AT LEAST TWICE EACH DAY. PICKING HAND MUST BE ON THE BRIDGE OF YOUR GUITAR. PICK STRINGS WITH YOUR PLECTRUM FROM HERE ON. KEEP PRESSING HARD AND TRY TO MOVE YOUR FINGERS TO THE CORNER OF EACH FRET.

7. RHYTHM EXERCISES   PRACTICE STRUMMING USING A PLECTRUM. MAKE SURE THE STRINGS ARE VAMPED WITH YOUR FRETTING HAND. STRUM FIRST OF ALL ON YOUR OWN, AND THEN TO YOUR FAVOURITE CD'S.

8. NOW REPEAT THIS EXERCISE WITHOUT THE PLECTRUM. USE YOUR THUMB FOR DOWNSTROKES AND YOUR FIRST FINGER FOR UPSTROKES.

9. NEW RHYTHM EXERCISE FIVE

10. CHECK THUMB POSITION ON CHORDS.

11. PRACTICE PIVOT FINGER CHANGES

12. THE MOON ROSE GUITAR CHORD EXERCISE

13. PLACE PLEC BACK BETWEEN THE STRINGS WHEN YOU FINISH.

14. FILL IN YOUR PROGRESS CHART.

MOON ROSE
GUITAR LESSON ELEVEN

THE GOLDEN SECRET

THE ART OF FAST CHORD CHANGING
THE GOLDEN SECRET
IT'S SO SIMPLE EVERYBODY MISSED IT
HOW TO PERFECT IT
A SIMPLE LEARNING TECHNIQUE THAT WILL HELP YOU PLAY THOUSANDS
OF SONGS
DIFFICULT CHORD CHANGES MADE EASY
ANOTHER INVALUABLE TEACHING AND LEARNING TECHNIQUE
HOW TO PERFECT G TO C
HOW TO PERFECT G TO D
HOW TO PERFECT D TO C

THE ART OF FAST CHORD CHANGING

The biggest obstacle of all to playing guitar is trying to get from one chord to the next. Here also lies the great difference between amateurs and professionals. If you are not quick, clean, and accurate, the song will never sound good. It also limits you greatly in the amount of songs you want to play.

WHAT YOU NEED TO DO TO CHANGE FAST

1. You only have a split second to change chords on guitar.
2. You need four good fingers, with all the skills shown to you in lesson four.
3. Your timing has to be perfect going from one chord to the next.
4. All fingers come off the strings at the same time (that's the easy bit, and land on the next chord at the same time (that's the hard bit).
5. Added to that you have to be absolutely accurate in order to produce a perfectly pitched sound.
6. And if that wasn't enough your timing has to be perfect with your rhythm hand also.
7. Then you have to do it all at the same time.

WHEN YOU SEE A PROFESSIONAL CHANGING CHORDS
IT LOOKS SIMPLE
WHEN A BEGINNER TRIES TO DO IT
IT IS IMPOSSIBLE

This is not shown to you in any other book, video or by most guitar teachers simply because they take these vital skills for granted themselves. They all show you chords and songs and assume that you then just go to D, or go to G, or go to C etc. In reality it is not that simple. It is also the reason why some teach yourself guitar books are not practical.

They are telling you what to play but what you really
need right now is to be shown how to play.

Then you will decide what to play. Why has no guitarist or book shown you how to do it. This is where our guitar books and workshops differ from all others. It is also the reason why our success rate is so high. A lifetime of teaching guitar has taught me that;

It is not enough to learn or teach chords on guitar.
We need to learn how to get from one chord to the next.

After all "The ability to change chords quickly is an art within an art".

If you have the patience to do the following steps well you will also make it look easy. They are simple and take a few weeks to perfect. The slower you can keep these learning techniques in the first week the faster you will be able to change once you have mastered them. If you can't do them slowly it is a guarantee that you can't do them fast. When you can do them slowly it is certain that your chord changes will become very fast depending on how much you practice.

Once you have it you will never lose it. All the techniques I am about to show you are exactly as played by professionals, and technically one hundred percent correct. It is impossible to improve on them.

THE GOLDEN SECRET
IT'S SO SIMPLE EVERYBODY MISSED IT

Can you take a close look at these pictures? They, like almost all songs played on guitar, have one thing in common. I have mentioned two songs here but I could include a million.

Intro
Harvest Moon
Neil Young

Changing
from one chord
to another

Intro
Whiskey in the jar
Thin Lizzy

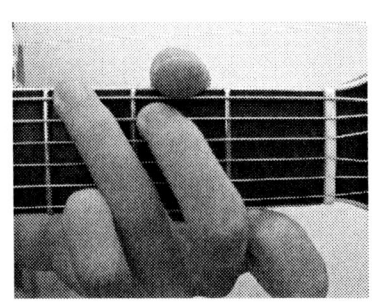

1. The third and fourth fingers move as one unit. They are together all the time.

2. They are the same relative to each other all over the neck of the guitar.

3. If you can move both fingers as one you are two thirds of the way to very fast chord changing.

4. This move is technically one hundred per cent correct. It cannot be improved upon.

5. It eliminates all unnecessary and waste finger movement. This alone speeds up your chord changes without doing anything else.

This is your starting point to really fast changing. It is your reference point for almost every song that was, or ever will be played on guitar. This skill also makes it possible to play guitar without looking at it, and without making mistakes.

If you have been playing guitar for a while and are still unable to change fast it is almost certain that you have overlooked this vital skill. You are not on your own.

I have never seen this properly explained by a book, video, dvd, or a guitar teacher. It is also one of the main reasons why I wrote this book. If you really want to be a good musician it is our responsibility as guitar teachers to make it as easy as possible for you to get there. It is my personal experience that the exercise I am about to show you is the key that unlocks the door to great guitar playing. I have seen it work thousands of times.

HOW TO PERFECT IT

A SIMPLE LEARNING AND TEACHING TECHNIQUE THAT WILL HELP YOU PLAY THOUSANDS OF SONGS

THE
MOON ROSE
GOLDEN FINGER EXERCISE

We will start by copying this picture.

- Can you position your thumb on top of the neck?
- Your second finger goes on the fifth string, second fret.
- Add your third finger goes on the sixth string, third fret.

POSITION ONE

Can you now very SLOWLY go to this picture.

- You must move both fingers as one unit down one string. They leave the first position together and arrive at the second position together.
- Your thumb does not move.
- It is not as easy as it looks.

POSITION TWO

- Can you now very SLOWLY go back up to position one.

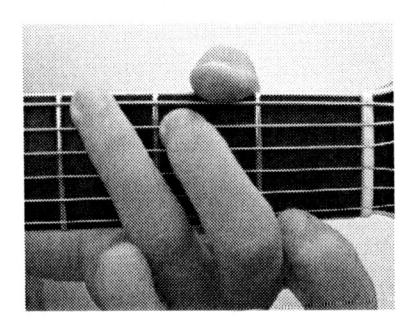

- Then very SLOWLY go down to position two again.

| YOUR THUMB STAYS TOUCHING THE SIXTH STRING AND DOES NOT MOVE |

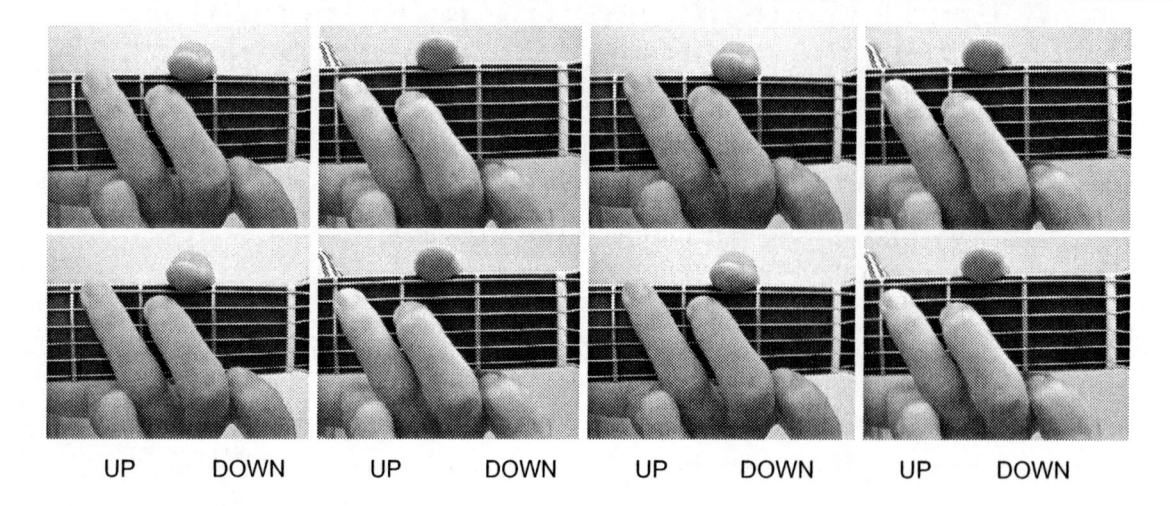

UP   DOWN   UP   DOWN   UP   DOWN   UP   DOWN

This is not easy to do at first. Every time you repeat this move it gets easier to do. Once you are able to move both fingers as one you will then be able to speed it up. You are also then two thirds of the way to mastering many chord changes on guitar. All we have to do is add an extra finger to this skill and we will have many full chord changes.

FOCUS POINT FOR STUDENTS AND TEACHERS

When practicing this exercise it is also very important to take the weight of the guitar under your rhythm arm. It will be hard enough for your fingers to change fast without having to take the weight of the guitar also.

It is equally important to have your thumb touching the sixth string second fret. The fingers should be doing all the work. This will ensure that the sound will be correct when we apply it to full chord changes. You will also be able to confidently play without looking at your guitar. The thumb stays in this position for practically all chords except E type chords where the sixth string sounds by slightly lifting the thumb. For younger students with smaller hands it is sufficient for the moment to have your thumb near this position. In time it will find its own way to the sixth string.

ANOTHER FOCUS POINT

Now is a good time also to eliminate all waste movement. This alone speeds up your chord changes. I have met many guitarists whose chord changing was not fast simply because their fingers were too much in the air going from one chord to the next. Let's compare these two pictures here.

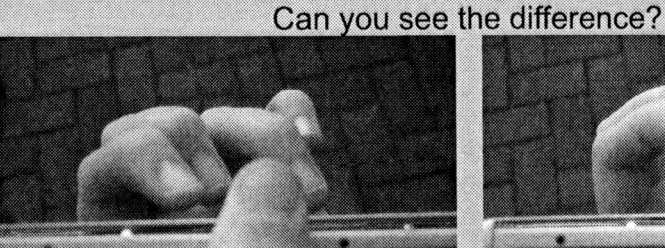

Can you see the difference?

YES   NO

These are two pictures of a guitarist going from G to D chord. Which is the better change? The one on the left. The fingers have been kept close to the fretboard during the change. The picture on the left shows a lot of waste movement and energy. It does nothing to promote good guitar playing. If this is you please change today. It will be uncomfortable for a day or two but I promise you once you have got used to it and applied it to all your chord changes you won't go back.

Like all the other lessons you can apply this learning and teaching technique for the rest of your life. Once you have got it you will never have to relearn it. It applies to all songs played on guitar.

DIFFICULT CHORD CHANGES MADE EASY

The most difficult chord changes to speed up when learning guitar is G to D, G to C, and D to C. They are also the most important because they are not in thousands of songs. They are in tens of thousands of songs, including many of your favorite songs. While it is easy to take the three fingers off G chord it is almost impossible to get them to drop onto D chord together. If you have been playing for a while have you noticed that your third finger is always last to go on the strings. It seems to be approaching the guitar from underneath the fretboard. Sometimes it even lands on the third string which gives a dreadful sound.

If you can copy what we are going to do here and are patient enough to practice it slowly and accurately I can promise you that the change from G to D will be easy in about four weeks. You will not want to go back to your old way of doing it.

ANOTHER INVALUABLE
LEARNING AND TEACHING TECHNIQUE

HOW TO PERFECT
G TO C

CHORD CHANGE

We will start by copying this picture.

- Can you position your thumb on top of the neck?
- Your second finger goes on the fifth string, second fret.
- Add your third finger on the sixth string, third fret.
- Add your little finger in the first string, third fret.

- Can you now very SLOWLY take your fingers just off the guitar, but definitely not up in the air. There is no music there.

- Can you now very SLOWLY go to this picture by moving your second and third fingers down as one unit.

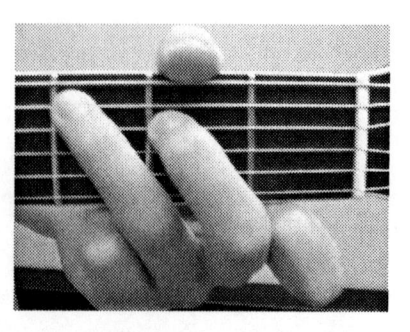

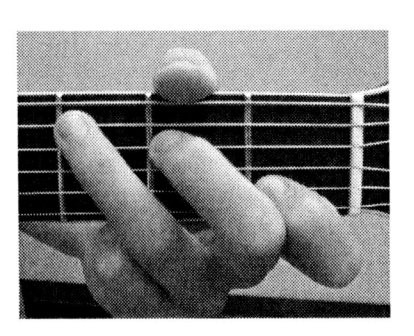

- Finally can you add your first finger onto the second string first fret. Now you have a C chord.

Now you will have to go back again and start with G. This is exactly the same as the previous exercise except that you add your little finger for G and your first finger for C.

It will be slow for a night or two as it feels as if it is the opposite of what you are used to up to now. Please hang in there. It won't be long getting easy. It is well worth the effort. Every time you do this the more you narrow the gap between yourself and a competent guitarist. Watch any professional player on tv or at a concert and you will quickly see that they are just doing a speeded up version of this.

HOW TO PERFECT
G TO D

CHORD CHANGE

THIS IS THE HARDEST ONE OF ALL FOR BEGINNERS
SO PLEASE PRACTICE IT SLOWLY

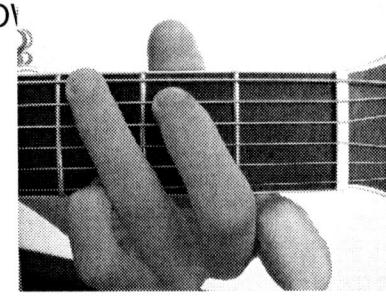

We will start by copying this picture.

- Can you position your thumb on top of the neck?
- Your second finger goes on the fifth string, second fret.
- Add your third finger on the sixth string, third fret.
- Add your little finger in the first string, third fret.

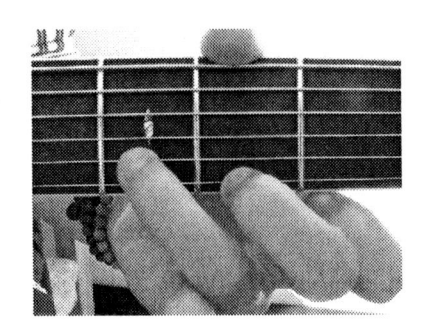

- Can you now very SLOWLY take your fingers just off the guitar, but definitely not up in the air.

- Can you now very SLOWLY go to this picture by moving your second and third fingers down as one unit.

- Finally can you add your first finger onto the third string second fret. Now you have a D chord.

Now you will have to go back and start again with G. This is exactly the same as the previous exercise except that you go to D instead of C.

HOW TO PERFECT C TO D
CHORD CHANGE

We will start again by copying this picture.

- Can you position your thumb on top of the neck?
- Your first finger goes on the second string, first fret.
- Add your second finger on the fourth string, second fret.
- Add your third finger on the fifth string, third fret.
- Can you now very SLOWLY take your fingers just off the guitar, but definitely not up in the air.

- Can you now very SLOWLY go to this picture by moving your second and third fingers down as one unit.

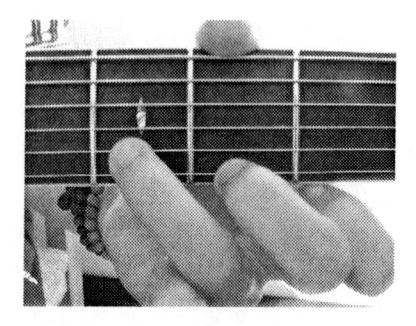

- Finally can you add your first finger onto the third string second fret. Now you have a D chord.

Now you will have to go back up to G and start again. This is exactly the same as the previous exercise except that you are going from C instead of G.

It takes about four to five weeks to perfect these changes. They are the hardest of all for beginners and you will need to practice them for a few minutes almost every day. Once you are skilled you will never have to practice them again. Even if you don't pick up the guitar for five years they will still be there.

FOCUS POINT FOR STUDENTS AND TEACHERS

Getting from G to D to C are the most difficult chord changes for beginners to perfect and the ones they need most help with. When a guitarist is changing correctly between these chords the fingers do all the work. THE THUMB NEVER MOVES. Can you look at these three pictures taken from behind the guitar.

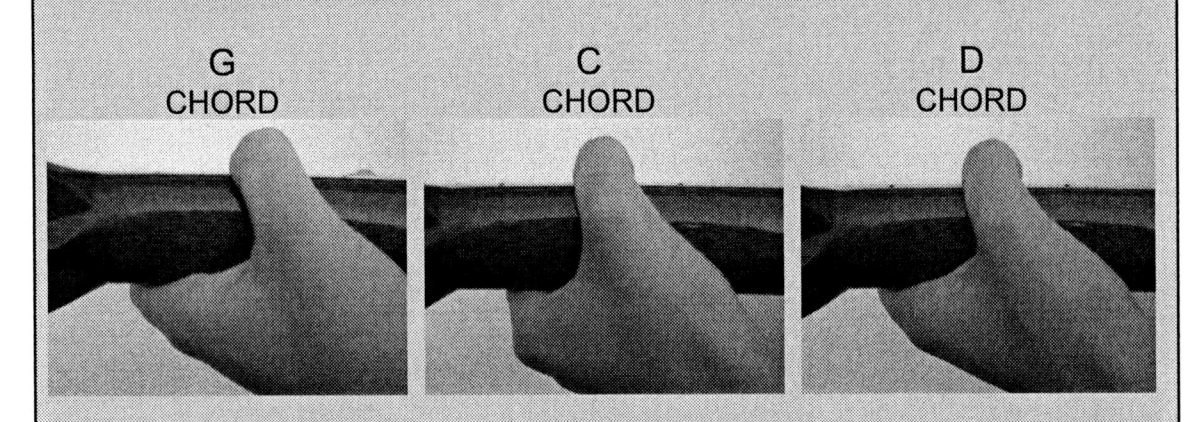

G CHORD   C CHORD   D CHORD

The thumb is the same in all of them. It hasn't moved. Once you have mastered this most other chord changes come to you quicker, except barre chords which take longer. You will be able to learn many songs by copying the chord pictures in this book and the best way to improve the chord changes for those songs is to practice with your fretting hand only from one chord to the next.

If you have mastered the golden finger exercise and implemented it to G, C, and D chords you have just acquired one of the great skills of guitar playing. It is in all styles of guitar from rock to flamenco and makes almost all songs much easier to play. Now the two biggest obstacles to playing guitar are behind you. Let's take the final step.

MOON ROSE

GUITAR
PRACTICE PROGRAM
LESSON ELEVEN

> ELEVEN VERY SMALL STEPS IS ONE VERY BIG STEP

1. CHECK YOUR SET UP   GUITAR SLIGHTLY TILTED BACK TO YOU

2. POSTURE CHECK   SIT TALL, HEAD UP, STRAIGHT BACK

3. THUMB EXERCISE 1   FIVE TIMES.

4. THUMB EXERCISE 2   FIVE TIMES

5. TUCK GUITAR UNDER STRUMMING ARM.

6. NEW FINGER EXERCISE 2   AT LEAST TWICE EACH DAY. PICKING HAND MUST BE ON THE BRIDGE OF YOUR GUITAR. PICK STRINGS WITH YOUR PLECTRUM FROM HERE ON. KEEP PRESSING HARD AND TRY TO MOVE YOUR FINGERS TO THE CORNER OF EACH FRET.

7. RHYTHM EXERCISES   PRACTICE STRUMMING USING A PLECTRUM. MAKE SURE THE STRINGS ARE VAMPED WITH YOUR FRETTING HAND. STRUM FIRST OF ALL ON YOUR OWN, AND THEN TO YOUR FAVOURITE CD'S.

8. NOW REPEAT THIS EXERCISE WITHOUT THE PLECTRUM. USE YOUR THUMB FOR DOWNSTROKES AND YOUR FIRST FINGER FOR UPSTROKES.

9. NEW RHYTHM EXERCISE FIVE

10. CHECK THUMB POSITION ON CHORDS.

11. PRACTICE PIVOT FINGER CHANGES

12. THE MOON ROSE GUITAR CHORD EXERCISE

13. THE MOON ROSE GOLDEN FINGER EXERCISE

14. PRACTICE CHANGING FROM G TO C

15. G TO D AND C TO D   FRETTING HAND ONLY

16. PLACE PLEC BACK BETWEEN THE STRINGS WHEN YOU FINISH.

17. FILL IN YOUR PROGRESS CHART.

MOON ROSE

GUITAR LESSON TWELVE

PUTTING BOTH HANDS TOGETHER

HOW TO PLAY SONGS
THIS SKILL IS IN ALL SONGS
A CHORD CHANGE EXPLAINED IN DETAIL
NOW YOUR GUITAR IS EASIER TO PLAY
NOW YOU HAVE IT ALL
GUITAR CHORDS BACK TO FRONT
THE BEST GUITAR CHORDS
BELIEVING IN YOURSELF
PROGRESS CHART

HOW TO PLAY SONGS

If you have come this far we are now ready to take the next step. That is putting both hands together. Do you remember what I said at the very beginning? All songs played on guitar come back to just three things;

1. GOOD CHORD CHANGES
2. GOOD TIMING
3. GOOD SOUND

In a lot of songs you strum a chord for four beats (called a bar of music). Then you would change to another chord for the next bar and maybe another chord for the bar after that. This is the approach we will use here to get you on the right road. Then you can try teaching yourself one of your own songs. As you progress you will discover that a chord may only last for half a bar of music or maybe a quarter bar. It is best for now to stay with full bar rhythms which is what you have been practicing in your programs up to now. After all we now have to put chord changes and quality sound on top of our rhythms. Once you have achieved this you look at things differently and be ready to take on more complicated rhythms and chord changes.

We will now take a few of the easier chord changes and try to put it all together. Let's take a look at the first chord change we perfected in lesson ten. Here it is again. The difference now is that you are strumming along with it too.

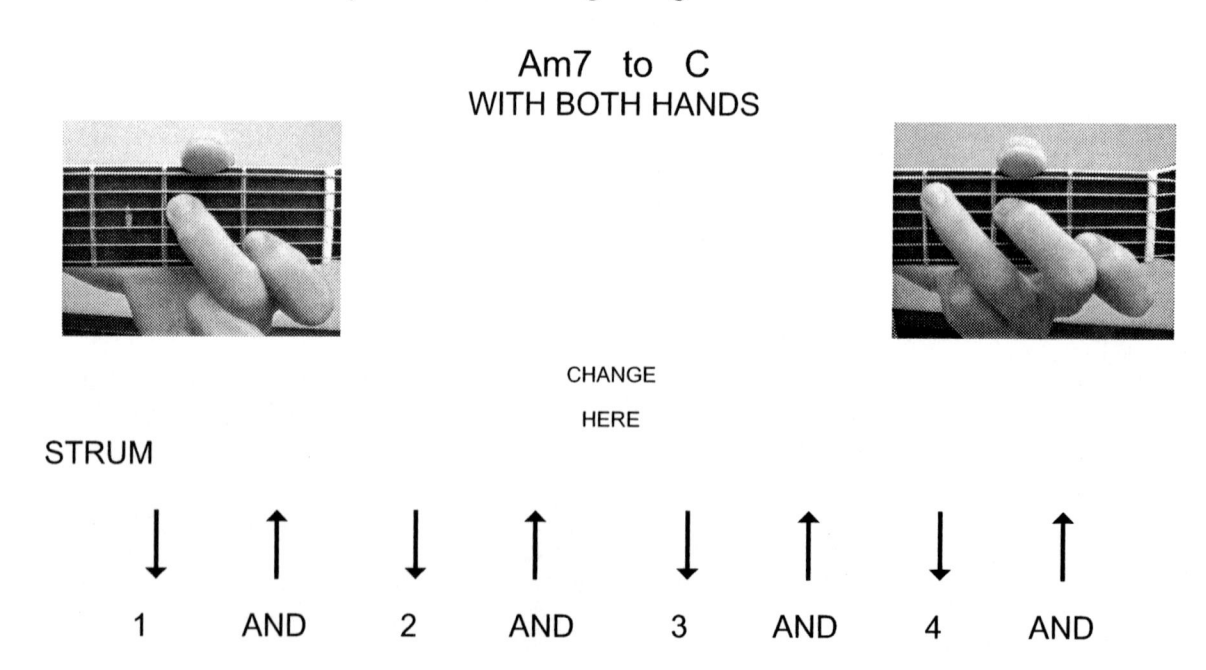

Am7 to C
WITH BOTH HANDS

CHANGE
HERE

STRUM

↓	↑	↓	↑	↓	↑	↓	↑
1	AND	2	AND	3	AND	4	AND

A to A7
WITH BOTH HANDS

CHANGE HERE

STRUM

↓	↑	↓	↑	↓	↑	↓	↑
1	AND	2	AND	3	AND	4	AND

Am7 to D7
WITH BOTH HANDS

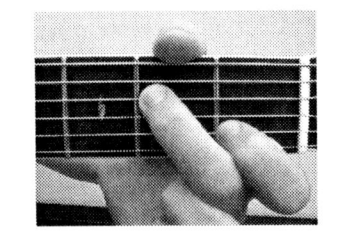

CHANGE HERE

STRUM

↓	↑	↓	↑	↓	↑	↓	↑
1	AND	2	AND	3	AND	4	AND

Em to E9
WITH BOTH HANDS

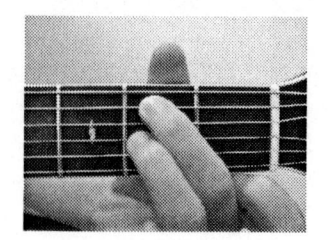

CHANGE
HERE

STRUM

↓ ↑ ↓ ↑ ↓ ↑ ↓ ↑

1 AND 2 AND 3 AND 4 AND

FOCUS POINT FOR STUDENTS AND TEACHERS

Playing with both hands together is a big jump forward if you are a beginner. Some chord changes only take minute to perfect. The more difficult ones like G, C, and D can take a month to perfect.

If you rush this vital stage you will lose your quality. That is why it is better when you start to play with both hands together to focus on pivot finger changes first. You will quickly perfect these. They will give you the feeling inside of what we call continuity. This is the ability to change from one chord to the next without having to stop. You are now able to change and keep good time with your rhythm hand.

Once you have achieved this, the feeling of continuity will then gradually transmit itself to the more difficult chord changes and a few weeks later you should be able to play them too without stopping. Then you are ready to correctly teach yourself and play thousands of songs from song books and the internet.

The following skill will help beginner guitarists greatly. I have never seen it in a teach yourself guitar book and I don't know why. It is vitally important to students and both their ability to change and sound quality almost instantly. I have seen this one skill make the difference between a student succeeding and failing. I am not talking about once or twice either. I have personally witnessed this thousands of times. I couldn't call myself a guitar teacher if I wasn't making you aware of the next skill. Based on a life time of personal experience teaching guitar I would not rate this book as a teach yourself guitar guide without the next technique. It is in all songs.

THE
MOON ROSE
GUITAR
PEDALING TECHNIQUE

THIS SKILL IS IN ALL SONGS

YET AGAIN IT'S SO SIMPLE …..THEY ALL MISS IT

There is an invisible skill in all guitar songs that you will miss if it is not pointed out to you. Many professionals do it and are not even aware of it. It is the ability to pedal from one chord to the next. If you are having difficulty trying to change this will help you a lot simply because it is actually easier to do. We all overlook it because it is invisible. IN A SONG IT HAPPENS TOO FAST FOR THE NAKED EYE TO PICK IT UP.

A CHORD CHANGE EXPLAINED IN DETAIL

A BAD CHORD CHANGE

Most teaching methods give a beginner the impression that you complete a strum pattern for a bar of music, then change to the next chord, and then start the next measure and so on. This creates three big problems;

1. It causes a very bad sound on the first strum of the next chord.

If this is you, you will notice that your sound is only coming right on the second beat of the bar. You never can get a quick change and a clear sound straight away.

2. You are trying to change so fast that it puts a jerk type feeling into your guitar playing.

When this happens you feel as if you have to stop at the end of each bar before you can start strumming the next chord.

3. It is impossible to do.

I more than most respect that all guitar teaching methods are there with the greatest of intentions. The problem is that the way most of them are interpreted is actually impossible to do. I tried it and I couldn't play a song smoothly. So what chance has a beginner?

A GOOD CHORD CHANGE

Chord changing happens during the last half beat of a bar of music. It does not happen on the first beat of a bar of music as many of us are led to believe. There is a big, big difference between the two.

I have made sure all the rhythms in this book end with upstrokes to give you the best possible chance to ingrain this skill into your guitar playing and as quickly as possible.

Here is a quick way to perfect this. Can you go back to the Em to E9 change we strummed earlier in this lesson?

This time strum   **Em**

DOWN, UP DOWN, UP DOWN, UP, DOWN, AND DURING THIS LAST UPSTROKE MOVE YOUR THIRD FINGER DOWN TOWARDS THE THIRD STRING.

Then strum   **E9**

DOWN, UP DOWN, UP DOWN, UP, DOWN, AND DURING THIS LAST UPSTROKE MOVE YOUR THIRD FINGER UP TOWARDS THE SECOND STRING.

Keep repeating this for a minute. Then stop.

NOW YOUR GUITAR IS EASIER TO PLAY

1 Did you notice how much better your guitar now sounds?

2 Did you notice how much easier this is to do than what you might have been doing?

3 Did you notice how much more enjoyable this way of playing is?

4 Did you notice that you seem to have more time to get it right? All the great players seem to have lots of time on their guitar. In other words they are not under pressure.

THIS IS YOUR
INTRODUCTION TO PEDALING

You are getting results quickly here because you are using pivot finger changes. It would be a good idea now to practice more of these type changes before moving on.

FOCUS POINT FOR STUDENTS AND TEACHERS

The most difficult changes for a student to perfect are G, C, and D. They are also some of the most important because they are in so many thousands of songs. Because of this they will take up a lot of your practice time but only for the next few weeks. Once you are over this hurdle you have them for life. You will actually be able to play rhythm guitar to thousands of songs without learning anything else on the guitar if you don't want to. This includes some of your own favorite songs.

To make sure you stay on the right road while speeding up these changes I have illustrated the G to D change here as clearly as I can. Once you have got this particular change your fingers will tend to subconsciously copy this approach when you are practicing most other chord changes.

The golden finger exercise combined with pedaling are the two crucial skills of good chord changing.

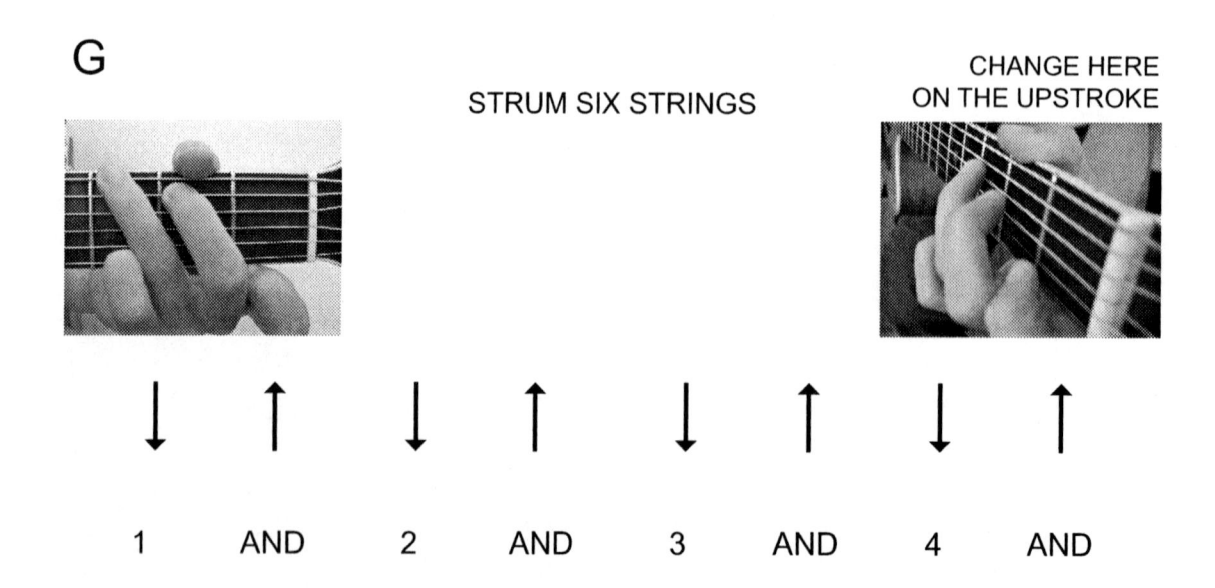

G

STRUM SIX STRINGS

CHANGE HERE ON THE UPSTROKE

↓　↑　↓　↑　↓　↑　↓　↑

1　AND　2　AND　3　AND　4　AND

D

STRUM SIX STRINGS
THUMB STAYS TOUCHING TOP STRING

CHANGE HERE ON THE UPSTROKE

↓ ↑ ↓ ↑ ↓ ↑ ↓ ↑

1   AND   2   AND   3   AND   4   AND

FOCUS POINT FOR STUDENTS AND TEACHERS

YOUR LITTLE FINGER

One of the biggest obstacles to mastering a quick change to G is your little finger. It jumps up in the air and then you have to bring it all the way down to the first string again. If you pick up your guitar and watch your little finger while changing from D to G you will see what I am pointing out.

Any kind of waste movement like this makes chord changing difficult. The fastest way to eliminate this is as follows.

Form a D chord.
Before you change to G hold your little finger down near the first string with your other hand.
Now change to G chord with your second and third fingers while pushing your little finger down on the first string.
If you do this a few times every day your little finger will eventually find its own way directly to the first string. Just now it is not independent enough.

To help you speed up your chord changes even more can you take a look at these two pictures. You can change either ways. The first way is amateur. The second way is professional. Your fingers are much closer to the fret board as they move from chord to chord thus eliminating all waste movement.

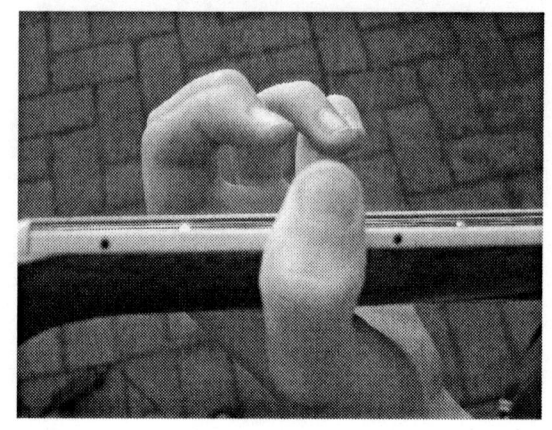

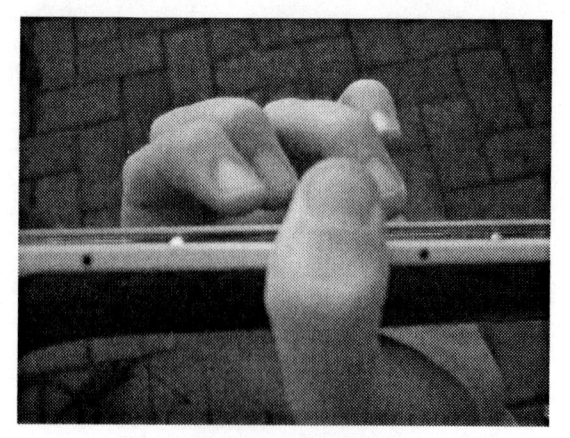

Amateur   Professional

YOUR THUMB

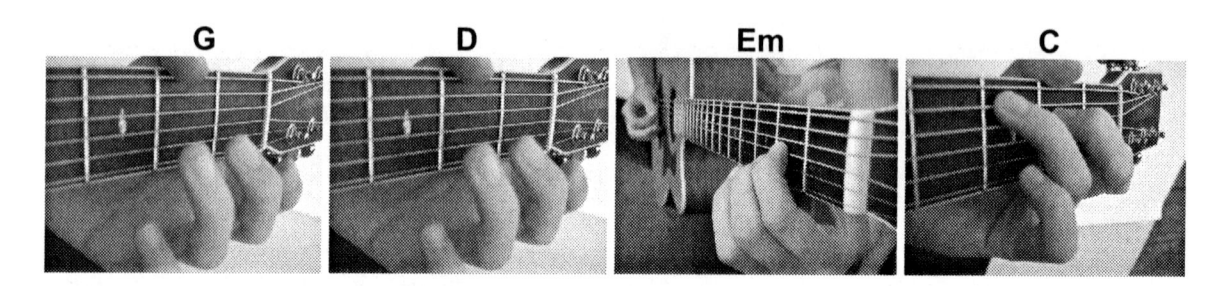

G   D   Em   C

FOCUS POINT FOR STUDENTS AND TEACHERS

Do you remember at the very start of this program I said that without good thumb positioning good guitar playing is impossible? Well even if your fingers are technically one hundred per cent correct and your changes are super fast your guitar still won't sound right if the sixth string is sounding freely on most chords. It gives off that dreadful booming noise that all beginners get when they first strum a guitar. The thumb mutes the sixth string on all chords except E type chords. This applies to every song that ever was recorded or ever will be recorded.

NOW YOU HAVE IT ALL

The ability to pedal combined with the golden finger exercise guarantees that your chord changes are always fast and accurate. However it is your thumb that guarantees that you always have a clear and professional sound. It is my experience that it takes most guitar students three to five weeks to perfect these vital skills.

GUITAR CHORDS
BACK TO FRONT

PLEASE LOOK AT YOUR THUMB POSITION
CAREFULLY BEFORE YOU LEARN A CHORD

FIRST YOUR THUMB……………….………..THEN YOUR FINGERS

With the chords in this book, a capo, and the guitar rhythms in this book you will be able to play not hundreds of songs, but thousands of songs. If you cant there are only two things stopping you from playing;
1, Your chord changing is not yet fast enough, or
2, Your sound is still not clear.

If this is happening please go back to lessons eight and nine. Read them again carefully and follow the practice programme. In time they will speed up your changes and brighten your sound. Do you remember what I said at the start of this book? These are the two biggest obstacles to playing guitar.

I have enclosed two thumb positions here to remind you again of the importance of thumb positioning. If you tried to learn guitar before and found it difficult or almost impossible to play it is almost certain that you focused so much on fingering that you forgot about the importance of what happens behind the guitar. We have got everything exactly right in these pictures. Please look at your thumb position carefully before learning a chord.

Without good thumb positioning it is impossible to play guitar.

THE BEST GUITAR CHORDS

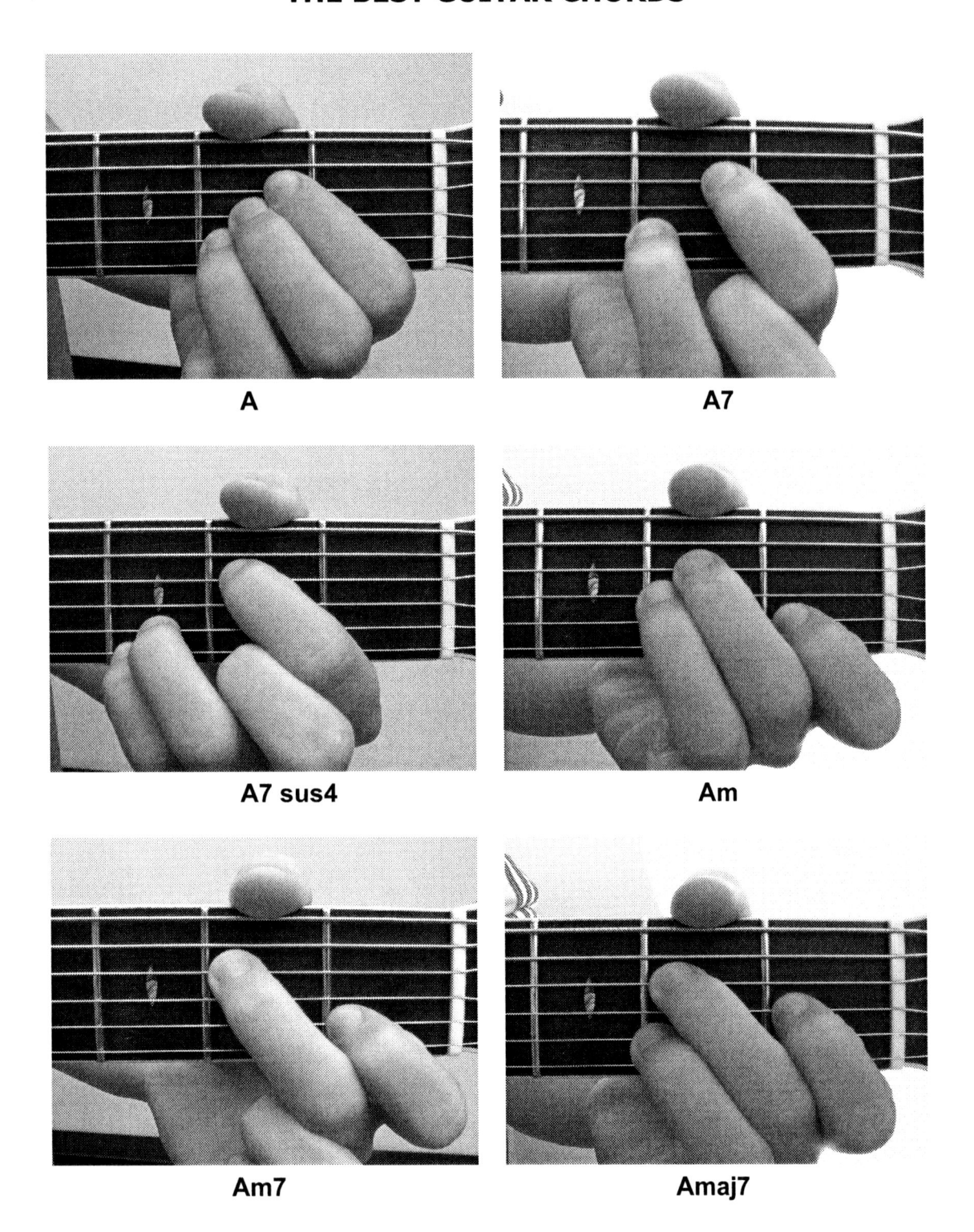

A

A7

A7 sus4

Am

Am7

Amaj7

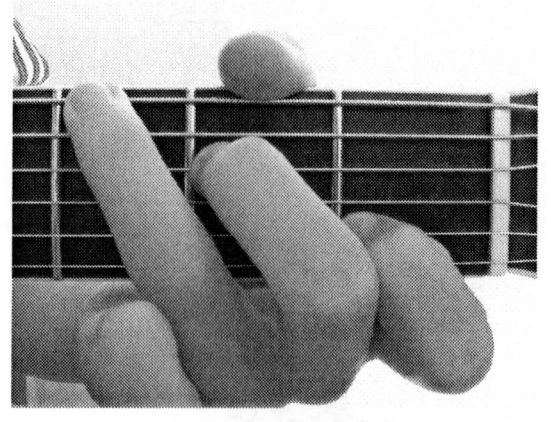

Am7 add G  **B5**

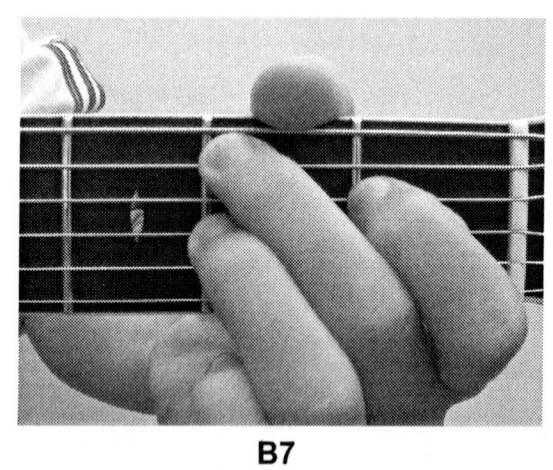

B7  **Bm**

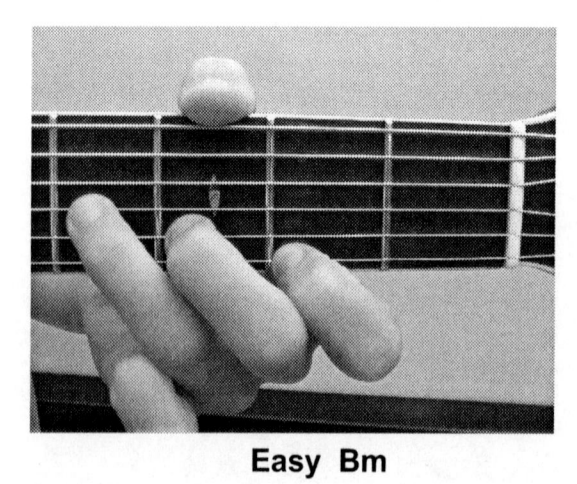

Easy Bm 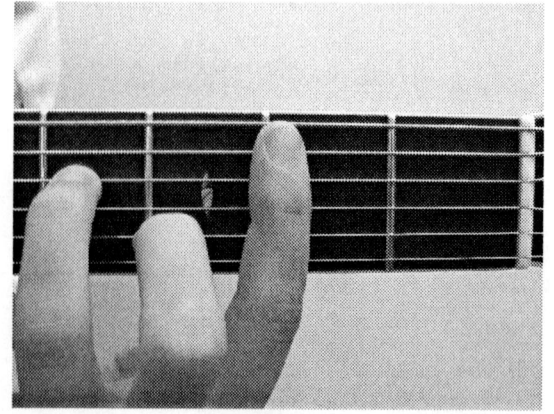 **Bm7**

C	C add9
C maj7	D
D7	DaddB

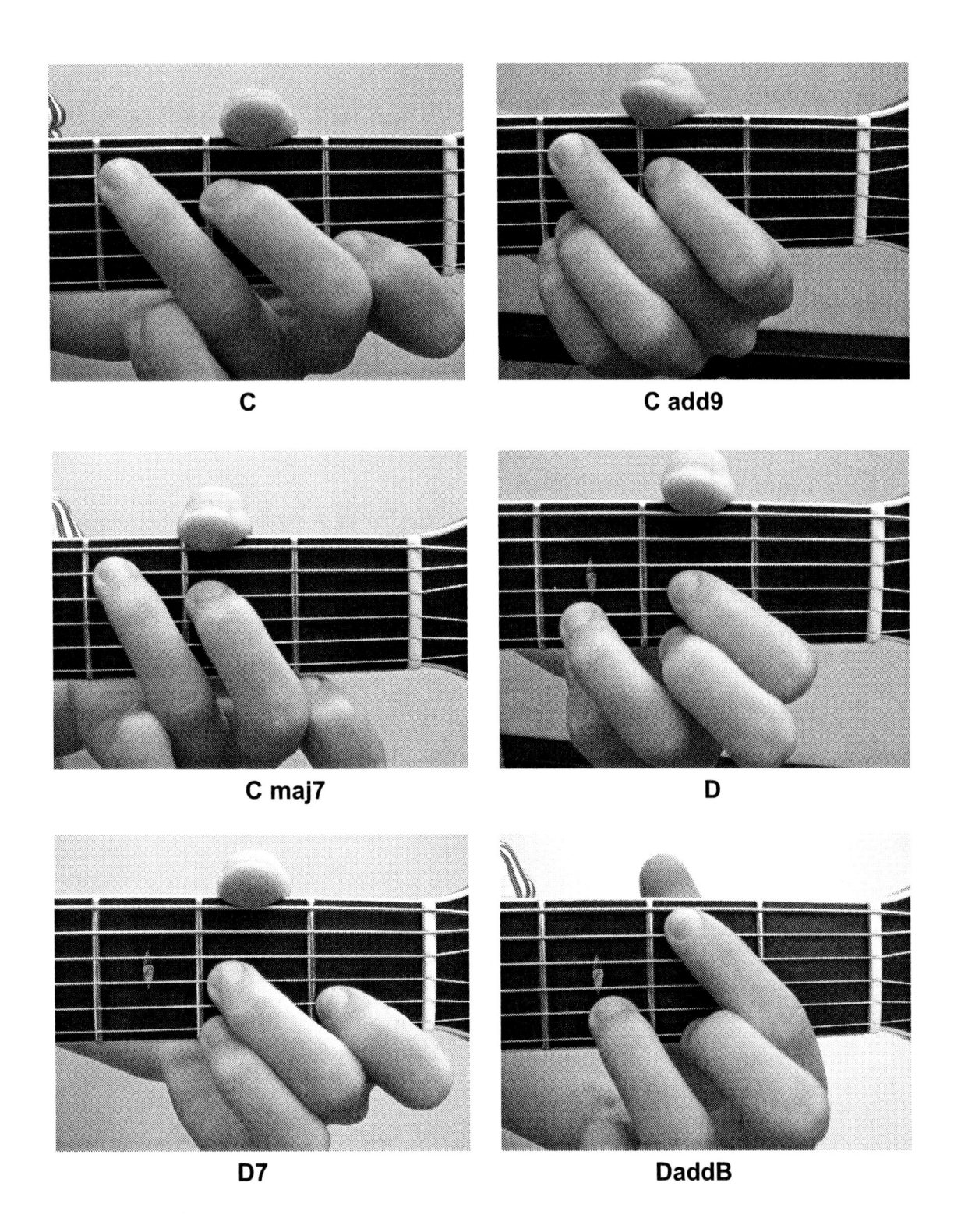

D sus2

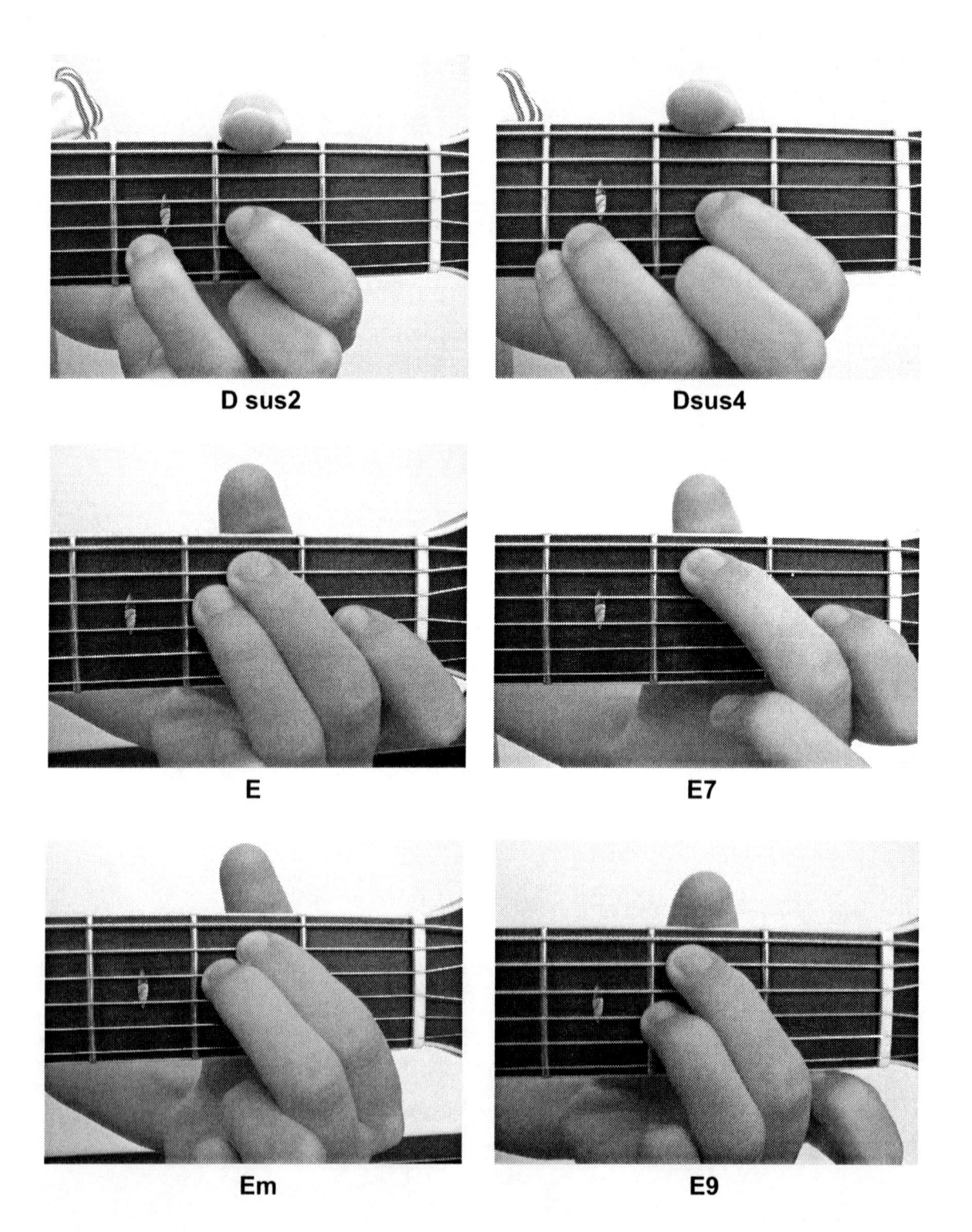

Dsus4

E

E7

Em

E9

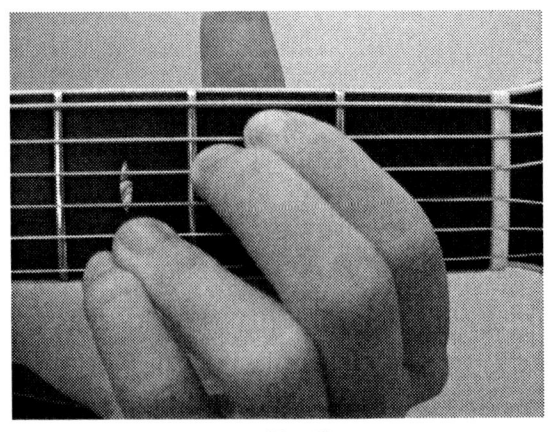

Em7

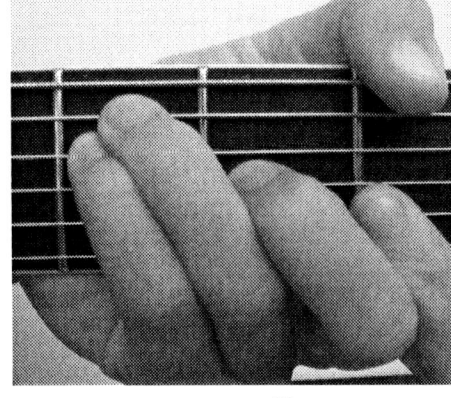

F

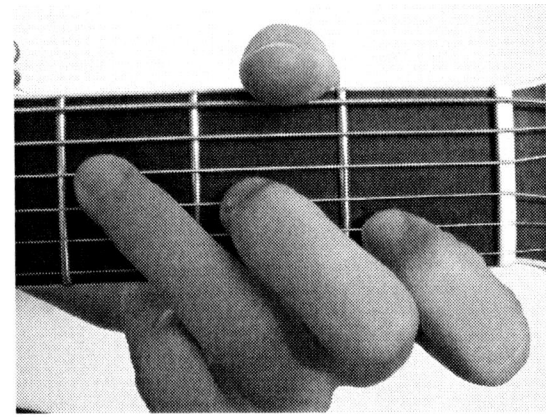

F maj7

G ADD F#

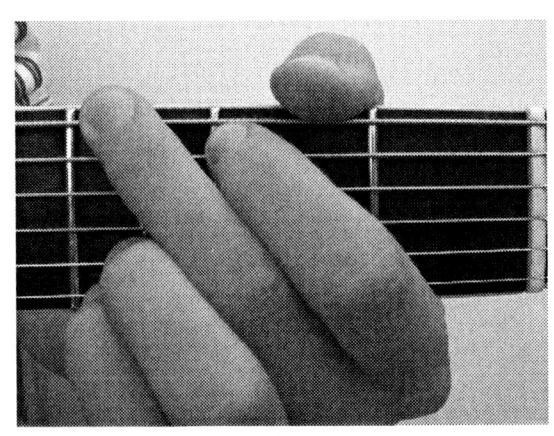

G 1

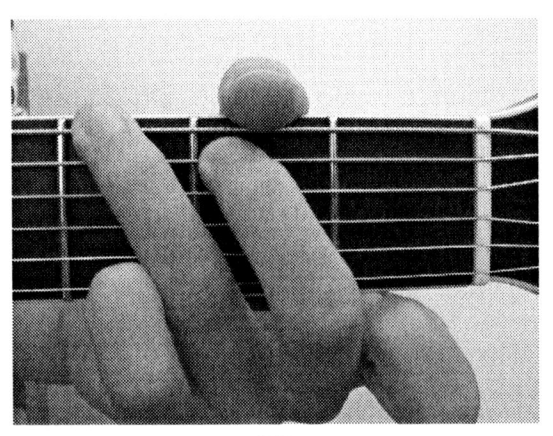

G2

BELIEVING IN YOURSELF

*There is no such thing as failure
when it comes to learning guitar.
You are a success because you tried.*

If you do not believe that you can become a good guitarist in the beginning, don't worry. You are not on your own. Most people don't, especially adults. Do you remember Seamus McKenna's letter at the start of this book.

It has always been my experience as a guitar teacher that enhancing a students self esteem is one of my most important tasks when they start. It is equally as important as learning how to play, and far more important than learning what to play. Looking back now over the thousands of guitar classes I have done, their belief in the beginning was the one thing that ensured the success of their journey on guitar.

Here is a learning technique that is so simple and yet helps hugely in this regard.

WRITE IT DOWN ON PAPER

The only people who have disagreed with me are those who haven't tried it.
It is a great idea to keep a record of your practice sessions from day one. Because improving on guitar happens in slow motion and is almost invisible we sometimes cannot see the progress we are actually making. Many of us tend to think about what we can't do rather than what we can do. Keeping a record lets us see the progress we are making. It keeps us on the right track, and helps to clarify our thinking.

As I said at the start if you are a beginner I have kept you in the forefront of my mind all through writing this book. To help you further with believing in yourself all the steps and learning techniques are small and manageable.
I have also included a progress chart to help you see how well you are doing.

When we work in steps that are too big we fail. When we learn in small steps we always succeed and move onto the next. It enhances our self esteem. Then we start really believing. Ten small steps is one big step on guitar.

FOR GUITAR TEACHERS

Another great benefit of the progress chart is that it helps guitar teachers to pinpoint each student's strengths and weaknesses. One of the reasons we practice is to make our greatest weakness our greatest strength. It also gives us a clear mental picture of the areas we need to improve with each student. It is my personal experience that most of the time **guitar students who use this chart improve much quicker than those who do not use it.**

MOON ROSE
GUITAR
PROGRESS CHART

WHAT GETS MEASURED GETS DONE

It is a good idea to fill in this chart once a week, or ask your guitar teacher to help you with it. Obviously you will not be able to fill in all the boxes in the early weeks. Scoring yourself marks out of ten and then adding up your total is probably the simplest and best system. Your aim is to try to improve your score each week. When you look back after the ten lessons in this book you should be amazed with your progress.

MOON ROSE

GUITAR

PROGRESS CHART

GUITAR	WEEK 4	WEEK 5	WEEK 6	WEEK 7	WEEK 8	WEEK 9	WEEK 10
POSTURE / SET UP							
4 FINGER EXERCISE							
RHYTHM EXERCISES							
THUMB EXERCISES							
2ND + 3RD FINGER EXERCISES							
CHORDS							
SOUND QUALITY							
SPEED CHANGING							
PIVOT CHANGING							
G TO D CHORD CHANGE							
G TO C CHORD CHANGE							
C TO D CHORD CHANGE							
STRUMMING WITH CD's							
RIGHT HAND ON BRIDGE							
FINGER PICKING							
BOTH HANDS TOGETHER							
INVISIBLE TRIANGLE							
TOTAL							

MOON ROSE

GUITAR
PRACTICE PROGRAM
LESSON TWELVE

> BELIEVE AND SUCCEED

1. CHECK YOUR SET UP — GUITAR SLIGHTLY TILTED BACK TO YOU

2. POSTURE CHECK — SIT TALL, HEAD UP, STRAIGHT BACK

3. TUCK GUITAR UNDER STRUMMING ARM.

4. NEW FINGER EXERCISE 2 — AT LEAST TWICE EACH DAY. PICKING HAND MUST BE ON THE BRIDGE OF YOUR GUITAR. PICK STRINGS WITH YOUR PLECTRUM FROM HERE ON. KEEP PRESSING HARD AND TRY TO MOVE YOUR FINGERS TO THE CORNER OF EACH FRET.

5. RHYTHM EXERCISES — PRACTICE STRUMMING USING A PLECTRUM. MAKE SURE THE STRINGS ARE VAMPED WITH YOUR FRETTING HAND. STRUM FIRST OF ALL ON YOUR OWN, AND THEN TO YOUR FAVOURITE CD'S.

6. NOW REPEAT THIS EXERCISE WITHOUT THE PLECTRUM. USE YOUR THUMB FOR DOWNSTROKES AND YOUR FIRST FINGER FOR UPSTROKES.

7. NEW RHYTHM EXERCISE FIVE

8. CHECK THUMB POSITION ON CHORDS.

9. PRACTICE PIVOT FINGER CHANGES

10. THE MOON ROSE GUITAR CHORD EXERCISE

11. THE MOON ROSE GOLDEN FINGER EXERCISE

12. PRACTICE CHANGING FROM G TO C

13. G TO D AND C TO D — FRETTING HAND ONLY

14. PRACTICE PLAYING SONGS WITH BOTH HANDS TOGETHER.

15. PLACE PLEC BACK BETWEEN THE STRINGS WHEN YOU FINISH.

16. FILL IN YOUR PROGRESS CHART.

If you have thoroughly followed the twelve lessons, the practice programs, and completed the progress chart

Congratulations

Now You Can
Play Guitar

NOW YOU CAN PLAY GUITAR

If you have got this far you have done really well. Can you think back to when you first opened this book? If you have followed each lesson thoroughly you have come a long way.

Now you can play guitar. There are no shortcuts to anywhere worth going. I don't believe in them. But I do believe in multi-tasking. I am going to share with you another secret. It will be of great benefit to some of you either now or in the future.

I never learned to play banjo but I always wanted to. My flat mate in London, John Gallagher had a six string banjo. Because of the lightness of the strings and their gauge it had to be tuned differently. If I tried to tune it like a guitar I would have broken all the strings.

One night I had an idea. I noticed that the strings were very similar to electric guitar strings. While John was out I took the strings off his banjo. Then I took the strings from my electric guitar and put them on his banjo. Then ……..

BINGO……NOW I COULD PLAY BANJO TOO

In a few minutes I had achieved one of my life-long dreams. And I did it without ever taking a lesson or practicing. Now all the chord positions and notes on the six string banjo were exactly the same as guitar. Later that night John came in. He nearly got sick. He could not believe what he was hearing. Then, to try and even up the score, he had an idea. He tried my idea in reverse to see if he could learn guitar as quickly as I learned banjo. It didn't work. This time he got sick.

CAN YOU SPOT THE DIFFERENCE?

THERE ISN'T ANY.

Have a look at the two photos here. In the first one I am playing my guitar and in the second I am playing my banjo. When I play in sessions or with groups most people that know me come up and say "Oh I didn't know you played banjo too. You must be gifted". Was it hard to learn? I say "Oh yes very hard", and then politely excuse myself.

If they had taken a closer look as we are going to do now they would have seen that there was no difference whatsoever between the two, except for the way each instrument looks and sounds. Both of them have slim necks, six guitar strings, the same fret board layout, and I am playing a G chord in both pictures.

All the skills I have shown you in this book are exactly the same for six string banjo as for guitar. You didn't expect that did you? If you have thoroughly followed each lesson

NOW YOU CAN PLAY BANJO TOO

One of the greatest compliments I ever got was when I heard that my teaching and learning techniques were being used for banjo and mandolin also. I never expected that.

Please remember to take the strings off and fit a set of electric guitar strings on the banjo instead. Once they are in tune you can play everything you learned on the guitar on the banjo.

THE INVISIBLE TRIANGLE

THE ONE GUITAR SKILL THAT ALL THE GREAT PLAYERS HAVE

I have been asked the following two questions thousands of times.
Why good guitarists make it look so easy to play?
What above all others would I consider to be the greatest skill a guitarist could have?. The answer to both questions is the same. I call it "The Invisible Triangle".

In this picture can you take a close look at the gap between the bottom of the fretboard and the base of the fingers? Notice how far away the base of the little finger is compared to the first finger. This is what we visualize as "The Invisible Triangle".

Can you see the invisible triangle here? It creates room for your fingers to move quickly and easily

If you lose the triangle your fingers have no room to move freely.

This is the best hand position from which to build most chords with your fingers. It is vital that you hold this angle and let your fingers come up to the guitar. You will very quickly get into difficulty if you move your hand up to put the fingers in place.

ONE SIMPLE GUITAR SKILL TRANSFORMS EVERYTHING

If you can hold as much of this angle as possible while you are fingering chords, (EXCEPT F AND BARRE CHORDS) or changing from one chord to another you will find playing guitar much easier once you are used to it. It is when we lose this space that chord changing feels uncomfortable and looks like hard work. If you are somebody who has been playing for a long time but you still find some chord changes difficult it is highly likely that your hand is coming up too near the neck and not giving your fingers enough room to move freely.

I have shown this to thousands of students. They could hardly believe that a simple move like this transformed everything. Suddenly the fingers moved quickly and easily from chord to chord, the thumb stayed in the correct position on top, and the sound improved because the first string was not being muted any more. Having studied many great guitarists I noticed that the invisible triangle was the one thing they all had in common.

This would also explain why some people improve quicker than others when they start. Many guitar students accidentally start this way without realizing it but most of us (me included) start out by using our hands to move the fingers into chord positions and lose the invisible triangle.
The next time you are watching a professional guitarist on tv or in concert you will see exactly what I am trying to show you here. If you are doing it correctly your fingernails should be looking at your face on most open chords. If you look back at all the chord photography in this book we have been extra careful to make sure that this angle has been included for you to copy. It is in all the open chords except F in which case your hand will have to come up to the neck in order to play it.

WHY I WROTE THIS BOOK

I DID NOT WRITE THIS BOOK BECAUSE YOU CANNOT PLAY GUITAR.
I WROTE THIS BOOK BECAUSE YOU CAN PLAY GUITAR.

Learning guitar is like trapping a butterfly. If you reach out and try and grab a butterfly, all you succeed in doing is pushing him away from you. On the other hand if you do the right thing and wait what happens? The butterfly comes and lands on your shoulder. Learning to play guitar is like that. We have to keep doing the right things and wait. Time is capable of many things.

The ability to play guitar is a truly priceless gift. It is emotion. It lets your imagination roam. Even when words fail, music speaks. It cannot be bought, and yet unlike material wealth, once you have it, nobody can take it from you. Can you just imagine for one moment if everybody in the world was a musician? There would be no wars. Why? Because the world is our country.

These are a few of the many reasons why I wrote this book. First of all, I have never met another person anywhere in the world, who has worked with as many students or even one quarter of the amount as I have. This is not a boast. It is a fact. The teaching techniques and learning skills I have outlined in this book took me a lifetime to put together. I know they make a difference, a big difference. It has been a great privilege to see these methods help thousands of students learn and play guitar, and to watch them get better and better day after day. Whether you are a student or a teacher I know they will help you too.

It never ceases to amaze me that I still cannot find one guitar teaching book that clearly explains the guitar from both sides (front and back of the fret board). Everybody is so focused on the front of the guitar that they seem to have completely forgotten the fact that;

> If your thumb positioning is not correct behind the neck
> it is actually impossible to play guitar well.

If your thumb is correctly positioned behind the neck it becomes much easier to learn.

I still cannot understand why so many books and teachers show beginners how to play chords and then songs. They completely forget to focus on what they really need to know and that is "How to change fast from one chord to the next". It is like trying to put on a chain with a missing link. It falls off very quickly.

We have got you started on the right road here. The teaching and learning techniques in this book work. They get results. That's what Moon Rose Guitar Academy is all about.

If you have no knowledge of music whatsoever I have kept you very much in my mind all the way through writing this book. I have also done my utmost to write about the guitar in your language, and not that of a professional musician. Yet every playing technique is exactly as played by professionals. I have not compromised anywhere because on guitar half measures avail nothing.

While a great guitar teacher is hard to find he, or she is easy to recognize.
They are a lot of things, but a critic, certainly not. They teach you how to play, not what to play. They do not tell you how to play, they show you. I am often asked "What makes a teacher great"? Here is my answer. They are aware from the very beginning that if they treat a new student as if he or she were what they ought to be, they will become what they ought to be.

I have the utmost admiration for anybody in the world who teaches guitar. It is an art. Without you very little would be passed on to the next generation. I believe that the most important guitarists in the world today are our students. They are the future of our music.

You are welcome to try any of my teaching techniques in your guitar classes. I believe that they will compliment your own methods, which I am sure are very successful. If just one of these techniques helps just one of your students on their musical journey, I will be very grateful to have written this book.

It is my personal experience, having worked with over ten thousand guitar students of many nationalities, ages, and walks of life that these learning techniques have always worked. They are technically one hundred per cent correct. They cannot be improved upon, but please remember;

> Practice does NOT make perfect.
> Perfect practice makes perfect.

Every journey begins with a single step. If you are learning from this book you have already taken one of many steps on your own musical journey. I hope you get many hours of pleasure learning, playing, and sharing your music with your friends. You could send me an email at moonrose@eircom.net to let me know how you are getting on. I would be delighted to hear from you.

Thank you for your time and Good Luck on your musical journey.

Always the heart

Pauric Mather

WORLD GUITAR DAY

WWW.WORLDGUITARDAY.COM   WWW.SAMARITANSPURSE.ORG

Email worldguitarday@eircom.net

Not he who has much is rich
But he who gives much.

World Guitar Day was founded in Dublin Ireland, by brothers Pauric and Kevin Mather in 2004. It falls on November 1st each year. Its purpose is twofold.

1. To bring together guitarists of all ages, levels and walks of life, to share their musical skills and experiences.

2. To contribute to "Operation Christmas Child"

HOW YOU CAN HELP

On November 1st each year guitarists around the world are asked to give a guitar evening such as a performance, workshop or class to a group of people in their own neighborhood. There is no cover charge for these events. All you have to do is bring a "SHOEBOX GIFT" for Operation Christmas Child. It would make a great difference at Christmas time to a large number of our hurting little brothers and sisters worldwide.

OPERATION CHRISTMAS CHILD

Operation Christmas Child brings joy and hope to children in desperate situations around the world through gift filled shoe boxes. The program is run by Samaritans Purse which has been providing emergency relief programs for the world's poor, sick, and suffering since 1970. Operation Christmas Child provides an opportunity for all of us to be involved in a simple, hands on missions project while focusing on the true meaning of Christmas.

In 2004 Samaritans Purse collected 7,000,000 shoebox gifts worldwide and distributed them to children in 95 countries. Full details of "HOW TO PACK A SHOEBOX", and Operation Christmas Child, are available on Samaritans Purse website www.samaritanspurse.org.

After the event the shoeboxes are collected and brought to drop off points. From there they are distributed in countries suffering from war, poverty, natural disasters, disease, and famine. The shoebox gifts are given to children on Christmas Day.

Your contribution can make a difference.

Touching hearts

Printed in the United Kingdom
by Lightning Source UK Ltd.
112793UKS00001B/1-96